PURSUING GOD'S PRESENCE

PURSUING GOD'S PRESENCE

Disclosing Information

BILL VINCENT

RWG Publishing

Contents

I

My Personal Experience

Wow, I can't believe I'm sitting here right now typing this. The visions that God has given me throughout the previous few months have come as a result of these last few months. As I type, I look to the Lord and sense his presence all about me.

I am a regular guy who serves an exceptional God. If what has happened to me is as amazing as it appears, you can be sure it will be heavenly visits unlike any other.

Since 1991, I've been teaching God's Word. For many years, I have preached and ministered. People were uplifted as a result of personal prophetic ministry. My prophetic ministry has resulted in some healings and even a few of miracles. This may sound like the kind of ministry that ministers desire, but I was dead within. When I preached or worshiped the Lord, I felt nothing. I reached a point when I needed something new and fresh from God. In 2008, I pressed into God with the expectation of receiving something from Him. In many respects, I resembled a whiny youngster begging for a present from his parents.

I wasn't sure what was going to happen. I was looking for something new and exciting. There was a part of me that yearned for more of God. Tears were poured, and I screamed at God, telling Him that unless He gave me something new and exciting, I was done with ministry. I told God that I just had a few sermons left and that if I didn't get something new and fresh from Heaven, I'd be done. For days, this went on. I'd listen to music and yell for a while, cry for a while, and then lie in my bed waiting for the moment, which I didn't know how long it would take. There was still nothing, and the longer the deadness lasted, the more enraged I became at God, believing that if He didn't come up, I would be abandoned.

I was so lonely that I began to believe He wouldn't turn up. I cried, "God!" More than anything else, I require your assistance. I began to tell God that I loved Him and that I needed Him after saying, "God, I'm tired of this." I was crying in my room when the wind swept into the room, and I realized it was the King Jesus I was fighting for. There was no door open, no window open, and the air conditioning was turned off. I knew God had blessed me by allowing me to sense his presence.

That day, I felt like I'd been rescued in the desert after days without water.

I want you to know that I am aware of God's presence as I write this. As the Lord takes me back to remember, tears stream down my cheek. As you read this, I pray that presence overflows as well.

We've talked about how I discovered God's glory, but there's a lot more. As God directs, I may even repeat myself throughout this book.

I didn't want to stop there after feeling God's presence enter into my room and knowing God had visited me. I'd walk into my room around 8:00 a.m. every day and start pressing in. I'd turn on the computer and start listening to worship music in case God gave me something to write about. After an hour or two of praying in tongues and worshiping the Lord, I would feel the same amazing Glory I had had previously. This is something I would do every day for hours. After feeling God's presence, I would sometimes lie in my bed for hours, completely silent.

What began to happen to me has forever altered my life. I arrived at a location where I couldn't wait to get started. It seemed as though I and God were having a love affair. I've fallen in love with God. I'd dash up the stairs, like if I couldn't wait to be with Him any longer.

I'd hurry in, turn on the computer, and start blasting worship music over and over. God would appear every day.

One thing I noticed was that the more I performed it, the less pressed I had to be to experience the Glory. This must be given to you. I'd press in for hours before I sensed the presence. After a period of time had passed, I would press in for approximately an hour, and the presence of God would appear. Then, after a half-hour to fifteen minutes, God's Glory would appear. I opened my bedroom door to press in one day, and God's presence was already there. It seemed as if God had been anticipating my arrival. I didn't have to push for Him to show up. He had already arrived. This was one of those weeks. God of the Universe had been waiting for someone like me. He was as eager to be with me as I was to be with Him. WOW! Even if He was already there, I would go in and press my way in. More than anything, I wanted to please Him.

Many people have predicted the publication of this book. This is something God has been saying for a long time. This book is for everyone who loves God and wants to learn more about Him. The things I'm writing in this book, I believe, will work. A lot has happened since I found God in the way I did in early 2008. For nearly two years, I was the principal speaker at a Church Revival. This wasn't just any church; this was the one where I was a Pastor, leading Revival. The presence was all we had for the first several months of the Revival, and it was incredible. We persisted, and after about six months of revival meetings, signs and wonders started to appear. This was so out of the ordinary for me. Thousands of gemstones, gold dust, and multi-colored dust were available. All of this is a sign from God. Many individuals were healed, and miracles were performed. Cancers have been healed, tumors have been eliminated, and very extraordinary miracles have occurred, according to testimonies. A Word of Knowledge had been given to a little boy about a toe that looked like another toe. This young man was granted a miracle. You couldn't tell there was anything there at all. This is only one of many things God has done.

Some ministries have made it their mission to pray against God's will. They simply assumed the miracles and signs were not from God. They mistook them for demons. In this book, I will provide some scripture to support signs and wonders from heaven. I'm no longer the pastor of the church where the Revival took place. I've started a new ministry and feel more liberated than I have in the past. The major reason I'm confident that everything I've written in this book will work for you is that it has worked for me time and time again. God has been faithful at every fork in the road. I'm telling you, things will happen if you press towards God like I did. I'll have to say this: if you see God's glory and see his manifestations, there will be many who will claim it's not right. You'll discover who your true buddies are. I want you to consider this: even with all of the turmoil, one week in God's glory is worth it.

2

Soaking in the Glory of God

I'll tell how I came to be immersed in God's glory. We'll all learn how hunger is satisfied by a sense of God's presence and an encounter with Him that leads to a daily practice of God's presence.

These coming years, I feel, will be a great time for us to rise higher and go deeper in our connection with God. His lovely church, His heart longs for us to be in a close relationship with Him and to walk in holiness.

5:27 (Ephesians) "That he may present it to himself as a beautiful church, without spot, wrinkle, or any other flaw, but holy and without blemish."

It's time to enter God's embrace, pressing into His loving heart and allowing Him to convict us of sin so that we can be forgiven and cleaned. God is working wonders among us all. It will not be free of charge.

Revelation 1:9 He is true and just to forgive us our sins and purify us from all unrighteousness if we confess our sins.

Wow! We're on our way to becoming that immaculate, pure bride who will be a testament to His grace!

What happened to me in God's presence can be attributed to a time of several months spent soaking in Almighty God's presence.

When I encountered God in what I call the splendor liquid honey cloud of His presence, it was a moment of overwhelming visitation. For about a year, God blessed my prayer life, which ranged from one to four hours every day; all I could do was lie in His presence and be still. It was dubbed "soaking" by me.

All I was doing was getting out of my daily routine and seeking God. That's not to say I didn't want to. I recently discovered that in order to be in God's presence, I needed to remove myself from the hustle and bustle. I started by praying with a longing for God's power to bring me revival.

"Holy Spirit, please come," I continued begging. You claimed that if I came closer to you, you would come closer to me. You said I'd find you if I sought you out and searched for you with all my heart."

"God, I'm slamming into you with a vengeance. "I'm not giving up."

It was a desperate plea for God's presence, a desperate search. I was on a passionate search for the Lord, seeking His glory. It was a period of holy hunger and great tension.

I was desperate for Him as a person, and I was resolved to be more immersed in His glory than I had ever been. I desired to be immersed in His presence in a way I had never known before, and I resolved in my heart to have an encounter with Him unlike any other. I did everything I could to help. I spent hours praying in languages. I prayed, after all! I would make my demands known to God through praise, worship, intercession, and supplication. I was putting in a lot of effort and hoping for a breakthrough. I desired

God and was aware of His presence, yet I was never pleased with where I had been previously. I wasn't satisfied with what I'd seen. "Lord, I want more," I said. And I pushed my way in.

The fire, the passion, the newness, the adventure, and the excitement were all gone.

That was my state before I learned to soak, as I screamed out in holy anguish, yearning for God. That's how I learned about soaking. I discovered it when I was given the opportunity to press in, remembering God's promise that if I drew near to Him, He would draw near to me. "God of the skies and come down," I shouted in desperation. And he succeeded! He came down to show me that soaking is mostly about listening, waiting, and being silent.

Quietness has brought me more power and revelation in my walk with the Lord than anything I've done in prayer. I've realized that there is a space in the spirit where I feel the highest form of prayer can be found. It's a heartfelt silent prayer. Most Christians will never reach it because it is so high. They are unable to overcome the mental pressures. They fail to learn how to calm their minds and emotions so that they might experience authentic communion and friendship with the Lord via silence. We are not being quiet before the Lord in the church today. We don't get the concept of soaking and waiting. We don't use our spiritual senses or practice being in God's presence. We must learn how to enter the rest of God's creation. We have no concept of being still and knowing that God is God. We have no idea what it means to wait on God. I had genuine interactions with the person of Jesus Christ during my many months of learning to soak, which I shall discuss later.

I received a visitation from the Lord Himself at the conclusion of months of waiting, basking, bathing, marinating, and simply being in His presence.

I could feel his breath on my neck as he approached me from

behind. I know it was the Lord, and I desire for these kinds of encounters to happen again and again.

Now I'm going to share some thoughts that the Lord showed me regarding soaking and what it signifies.

1:5 in Acts For John actually baptized with water, but you will be baptized with the Holy Spirit not long after.

Believe it or not, there is a part of baptism that involves cooking and meal preparation. Pickles, BBQ, and even chili taste better the next day. It's as though God wants us to soak, and the more we soak, the more tastes we develop that resemble Him.

In Acts 1:5, the term baptize is translated from the Greek word abbath, which is derived from the verb bapto, which means to dip.

It contains the concepts of dipping, immersing, and submerging repeatedly, as well as being overwhelming (See the KJV New Testament Greek Lexicon)

Let's take a look at how to marinate a rack of ribs. When the ribs are marinated, they taste so much better. It becomes tender and juicy after soaking in the sauce for a few hours.

The process of marinating and soaking in the presence of the Holy Spirit are identical. That means being in His presence without thinking about ourselves, resting in His majesty, and allowing Him to fill us up. Keep in mind that Godly saturating takes weeks. It's possible that we'll need to soak for a long time before we're tender.

These word graphics may assist you in comprehending the biblical meaning of baptism.

Come and be in the river of my presence over and over again, says God's word. I want to completely immerse, submerge, and engulf you in my presence.

God encourages you to stay with Him until you've been transformed to the point that no one will recognize you when you emerge. God wishes to pickle us all. When I soaked in God's presence for months, I'm eternally grateful that God pickled me.

I emerged from the experience bathed with the Holy Spirit and His power, and I was no longer the man I had been. Soaking changed my life.

Similarly, I came to understand God's anointing, power, and miracles in the same way. By resting in solitude and silence in His presence, I was able to comprehend. God would speak to me and show me folks in the sessions as I sat in front of them. I take a seat quietly in front of the Lord. As I pondered His words, "Be still and know that I am God," I gained a deeper understanding of who He is.

"I release to you the revelation of who I am, and I cause you to know, I cause you to see, and I reveal myself in the stillness," God whispered to me in the stillness.

Quiet before the Lord is more difficult than you may suppose. Stillness is where revelation happens. It's waiting with bated breath, as if you're about to witness something. That's how I felt when I first started soaking. My mind and thoughts were focused on Jesus as I waited. Music was playing in the background while I waited. My entire focus was on Jesus. I drew my mind back in if it started to wander.

I encourage you to give it a shot.

I'd like to start by stressing the sponge and the water because, until we come into contact with the fountain source of live water, we can be like that old dried sponge.

Isaiah 58:11 is a prophecy from the prophet Isaiah. And the LORD shall continually guide thee, and satisfy thy soul in times of drought, and make thy bones fat: and thou shalt be like a watered garden, and like a well of water that never runs dry.

4:14 (John) But whoever drinks of the water that I will give him will never thirst; rather, the water that I will give him will be in him, a fountain of water springing up into everlasting life.

But pay attention. We won't look the same when the fountain of living water touches us, which can happen unexpectedly like an outpouring of the Holy Spirit. Like rivers of living water, God and His ways will pour out of us.

7:38 As the Bible says, whomever believes in me will have rivers of living water flowing from his belly.

Being dry, with the correct mindset, can be a motivator to press on and seek the Lord for an outpouring of His presence, companionship and protection, forgiveness, and cleaning power. So many times, the dry periods turn out to be the greatest!

I told you about my journey earlier in this chapter, how I was desperate and hungry for God, and how soaking in His presence began to transform me. We looked at a variety of cardiac problems, including hunger, thirst, and desperation. Everything of these attitudes lead to our hearts softening to the point where we yearn for God beyond all else.

So let's look at David because he recognized how holy desperation and devotion may provide us with the key to unlocking breakthroughs in our life.

63:1 (Psalm) When David was in the wilderness of Judah, he wrote this psalm. My soul thirsts for thee, my flesh longs for thee in a dry and thirsty desert where there is no water; to see thy power and grandeur, as I have seen thee in the temple. My lips will laud thee because thy lovingkindness is greater than life. I will bless thee in this way as long as I live: I will raise my hands in thy name.

My soul will be filled with marrow and fatness, and my mouth will sing praises to thee with glad lips:

David confesses his heart's longings here. He is aware of the Lord's lovingkindness. He was in the woods, fleeing from King Saul, when he wrote this Psalm. Don't miss out on this opportunity. David was making a prophecy when he said, "My soul shall be pleased as with marrow and fatness, and my tongue shall praise you with joyous lips." This assertion was the key to him receiving breakthroughs,

breakthroughs that would free him from that parched and desolate region.

This is the key.

He offered praise as a sacrifice.

13:15 in Hebrews As a result of him, let us consistently make the sacrifice of praise to God, which is the fruit of our lips offering praises to his name.

That is the secret to success. This is the key to discovering God. Going deeper requires this. And I'll be satisfied. I will be content. I can claim I'll be content because I know that if I seek You and thank You even while I'm thirsty, You'll satisfy me. Many believers today are thirsty and wandering in the desert. It may appear to folks in this scenario as though they are in the middle of a never-ending desert. Your desert experience will begin to be transformed if you can rise higher and dare to offer God the sacrifice of praise.

You won't be able to dwell in the wilderness indefinitely like David did.

12:1 in Hebrews Because we are surrounded by such a large cloud of witnesses, let us lay aside every weight and the sin that so easily besets us, and let us run the course that is set before us with patience, knowing that God is trustworthy and will see us through.

Take a look at what the Lord says via the prophet Isaiah.

41:18 Isaiah I'll make the wilderness a pool of water, and the barren land springs of water, by opening rivers in high places and fountains in valleys.

The ideal times to visit the desert wilderness are frequently when it is dry.

107:35 Psalms He transforms the desert into standing water and the parched land into springs of water.

Do you have any experience with the desert? A desert is a place for contemplation and solitude. The desert hints of a hidden location.

91:1 in Psalms He who dwells in the Most High's secret chamber will be protected by the Almighty's shadow.

Without the desert, you can't walk in God's power. I'd like you to know that we're well on our way to being that pristine, pure bride.

The true church, as you may know, is Christ's wife, and the bride must undergo refining in the desert, which includes sin conviction, forgiveness, and cleaning.

Purification is one of the benefits of being in the desert, as we discovered when we asked, "What else is nice about being in the desert?"

8:5 in Song of Songs That is this woman who appears from the desert, leaning against her beloved? I raised thee under the apple tree; it was there that thy mother gave birth to thee; it was there that she gave birth to thee.

That's us, true believers in Jesus Christ who love God whole-heartedly. Also, pay attention!

When we emerge from the wilderness, there is a specific time when we must return. However, the approach we take into the wilderness and the approach we take out of the wilderness are two distinct things.

Luke 4:35 And Jesus, full of the Holy Spirit, returned from Jordan and was led into the wilderness by the Spirit.

4:14 in Luke And Jesus returned to Galilee in the power of the Spirit, and a reputation for him spread throughout the region.

God wants us to understand that the path we take into the wilderness, or the desert, will not be the path we take out! He desires for us to have an outpouring of His Spirit in our life. We will emerge from the wilderness altered for the better if we keep the proper mentality! Did you know that when Jesus rose from the desert in the power of the Spirit, it was the appointed time for Him to chose His disciples?

I believe that once we have been transformed, both individually and corporately, as the bride of Christ emerging from the desert, we will be in a wonderful position to make vital judgments. There's even more!

I believe that as we emerge from the wilderness with an increase in the Holy Spirit, one of the first locations God wishes to lead us is to our own hearts, which will be flooded with a revelation of His goodness. He wants us to be filled with joy, as the wedding celebration at Cana symbolizes.

I feel that the location of the wedding party was also the location of His splendor! And we'll be able to be where His glory is when our hearts are full with joy and celebration. It's about God's Glory being able to surround us in the hidden area of our hearts. As a result, there is a divine purpose in our desert experience that is for our benefit. We'll learn to give God glory through sacrifice; we'll be purified and transformed; and we'll be in a wonderful position to make critical judgments in the desert.

Last but not least, God will lead us to a place of joy and celebration in our hearts, where His splendor can be seen.

5:6 Matthew Blessed are those who hunger and thirst for righteousness, because they will be satisfied.

Our hunger will be quenched! God longs for us to enter His presence and spend time with Him, to be with Him. When we immerse in God's presence, we get to celebrate and feel His glory. To shut out everything that drags us away from God and the secret place, however, we need the Holy Spirit's discipline.

Do you know what many pastors, leaders, and evangelists go through? They begin by soaking; they begin with zeal. They begin by being so in love with Jesus, so lovesick, that all they can think about is him from the moment they get up until the moment they go to bed. And the Lord's presence is new to them; they have "edge." The Lord's Word has an impact on their lives.

The phone starts ringing, and they get so busy with a mindset of giving, giving, giving, ministering, ministering, ministering, And then everything starts to happen.

But we must remain at the Lord's feet. There's something special about sitting at the feet of the Lord.

46:10 (Psalms) Be quiet and know that I am God; I will be exalted among the heathen and in the world.

What happens if we don't move? Knowing that God is God is a revelation for us. In this passage, the word know literally means "to perceive" (Strong's Concordance 3045).

It means to know via revelation, the same kind of revelation that convinced Simon Peter that Jesus was the Christ, the Son of the living God.

Matthew 16:13-17 When Jesus arrived on the Caesarea Philippi shores, he asked his disciples, "Whom do folks say that I am the Son of Man?" And they added, "Some claim you're John the Baptist; others say you're Elias; and yet others think you're Jeremias or one of the prophets." But who say ye that I am? he says to them. Simon Peter responded by declaring, "Thou art the Christ, the Son of the Living God." And Jesus replied, "Blessed art thou, Simon Barjona," saying, "For flesh and blood hath not revealed it to thee, but my Father who is in heaven."

We suddenly understand, perceive, and come to know God through revelation simply by being still and sitting in God's presence, not saying anything. Remember that David got a revelation of God's loving-kindness because he knew the Lord so well.

30:15 Isaiah For thus says the Lord GOD, the Holy One of Israel: "Ye shall be rescued in returning and rest; in tranquility and confidence shall be your strength," and you would not.

God's message of being in that calm area is shared by Isaiah. We can only gain confidence and strength by being calm and silent; then, God strengthens us. There is a location where you can obtain.

Mary, the sister of Martha and Lazarus, was mentioned by Luke, the physician, in his gospel narrative.

Acts 10:39 She also had a sister named Mary, who sat at Jesus' feet and listened to his words.

She put herself in a position of receiving and surrendering. She sat calmly, staring at His face and listening. In prayer, where do you stand? That is where God desires to lead us! Oh, how the Father yearns for our company—for us to walk humbly with Him.

Micah 6:8 is a prophecy by the prophet Micah He has shown thee what is good, O man; and what does the LORD want of thee but to do justice, love mercy, and walk humbly with thy God?

We can all enjoy God's presence. It will need you laying down your flesh. Soak in prayer and seek God for a deeper hunger and thirst for his presence.

3

Worship and the Blood of Jesus

Like no other time in history, we are on the verge of crossing a threshold in worship. There are a lot of things that have been kept until this last hour, with worship being one of the most important venues for the upcoming release. I understand that worship has only scratched the surface of what it is capable of releasing into the atmosphere, and that it will play a significant role in the release of the miracles and salvation that are going to be revealed on the world. I've never heard so many people who have actually found a heart of worship.

1:17 in 1 Corinthians For Christ did not send me to baptize, but to proclaim the gospel: not with wisdom of words, lest Christ's cross be rendered meaningless. For the message of the cross is folly to those who perish, but it is the power of God to those who are saved.

The Lord is speaking to me about Christ crucified. In my thinking, I keep coming back to the power of the cross and the blood of Jesus. There was a moment when I was through bible study. One of my teachers went into great depth about what happened on the cross. That day, it opened up a whole new world for me. I began to research in greater depth and discovered so much that it reawakened something inside me. The Passion of Christ is the closest film to the truth of what occurred to our Lord and Savior. To begin, consider that the ripping of His flesh had to expose his ribs and even organs due to the extent of the lashing. His visage had to be so distorted that they couldn't tell who he was.

So that His body could hang on that old tough cross, the nails had to penetrate through His wrists and ankles. It was rough handling of the cross that ripped Him open even more when they sat him upright. The cross was not as smooth as it appears in many images. The cross was rough, and Jesus would have had to pull Himself up to relieve the strain and obtain a breath when hanging on a cross like that.

It's horrible enough to consider the crown of thorns placed on His head. The significance of this detail, and believe me, there's a lot more. I feel something has been awakened in the hearts of those who sincerely receive a revelation of Jesus Christ's death. Keep in mind that Jesus was risen from the dead.

I pray for songs that depict it in such a way that no one can stand in the way of the revelation of Jesus Christ's resurrection power. All the melodies, all the poetry of words, all the reasoning, and all the understanding of man are nothing compared to the power of the blood.

I would encourage all worship leaders to seek the Holy Spirit's guidance in writing songs that provide insight and release the blood's power in the hearts of worshippers everywhere. 6:14 (Galatians) But God forbid that I should take pride in anything other than our Lord Jesus Christ's cross, by which the world has been crucified for me, and I have been crucified for the world.

One drop of Jesus' blood has enough power to make an atom bomb look like a small firecracker. We must enter into the revelation of the act of His blood being spilt for all mankind, so that nothing, not disease or infirmity, not even death, can stand in the way of its authority. In these final days, I think He will show the power of Jesus' blood.

We should start seeking the Lord on this and asking Him to provide the songs that would bring the glory of this revelation to the crowd.

63:2 (Psalms) To behold thy might and grandeur as I have seen thee in the sanctuary.

As we walk into that place of comprehending the power, I know in my heart that songs about Christ's blood and crucifixion will bring His glory into the room like nothing else. The Word made flesh in Jesus and His purpose on this earth brought the glory of God to the earth.

More praise songs are needed so that the entire body might join in with the hosts of heaven, giving Him the recognition He deserves for what He did on our behalf on the cross. 5:12 (Revelations) Saying aloud, "Worthy is the Lamb who was killed to receive power, riches, wisdom, strength, honor, glory, and blessing"

It everything comes down to the Lamb who was slain. We need to worship with a new understanding of the power of Jesus Christ's blood. The Church is no longer hearing enough about the blood.

Allow the revelation of His merit to be shown to us and to continue to unfold in us. Let the power of what He did on the cross be sung in our hearts and with our tongues, releasing faith that is ablaze with His glory into the sky. Allow the resurrection power of His shed blood to be released in our hearts, and let songs and worship about this truth fill the air. Allow it to bring the mass healings in worship that are on the horizon.

The sound of glory being given to Him in recognition of what

He did on the cross and what His blood has already achieved in terms of resurrection life has something to it!

That entails the resurrection of the dead and the healing of all ailments. The sound and songs must be written and released in order to fill the temple with His glory cloud. As we become one with Him in this reality being made evident, this revelation will inspire trust in everyone's hearts. Through and to us, the songs will release it in the assembly. Let it be, and let it be now, Lord.

It's time for such intimacy and revelation, which will be powerful in its own right. The Church can speak about the blood and even the power of the blood much too often. It was only available in Word. This type of worship will create an atmosphere conducive to healings and miracles, resulting in a harvest. God, we need your angels to release those songs that have been saved until this hour for the great last revival, causing the hearts of people to be healed physically, psychologically, and spiritually. Lord, may healings, miracles, and salvation occur in worship as we all sing the same songs with one voice and one sound, so that no one else receives glory but You. 12:11 in Revelations And they triumphed over him through the blood of the Lamb and the word of their testimony, and they did not love their lives until death.

Let us prepare ourselves to receive from the storehouse of heaven those songs stored for this time that testify of the resurrection power of the Lamb's blood, Christ crucified, and our witness of overcoming by that same power used in our lives. Oh, that the glory cloud would appear out of nowhere and fill the temple, so that no one could stand in the open presence of His glory as a result of this devotion rising as incense to His throne, inviting Him to come. Lord, come!

Intimacy With the help of the Holy Spirit

I'm going to tell you everything I've discovered in my quest to understand the Holy Spirit. I've developed a unique relationship with the Holy Spirit as a human. I'd like to share what I've done with you so that you can seek Him and make friends with the Holy Spirit.

I've had the privilege of living in contact with the Holy Spirit for the past three years. I'm going to give you some tips on how to discover Him in a way that very few people have. I hope my experiences inspire you to seek the Holy Spirit as well. It's past time for us to rekindle our interest in developing a connection with Him. I've had the privilege of living in the reality of one of the most magnificent communions with the Holy Spirit that you can imagine over the last couple of years. It feels so real to me, and I want it to feel the same way to you.

I'm hoping that my story will encourage you, no matter what position you're in, whether or not intimacy is taking place, and that you'll be filled with a renewed desire for a close relationship with Him. I'd like for you to be prepared for more. When I say "more," I'm referring to all aspects of God.

There is more to the Holy Spirit filling than merely speaking in tongues. Most of us have never experienced a deeper Holy Spirit intimacy. I want you to know that I can see that the Holy Spirit's person or presence has become as real to me as any man or woman anyplace I go today. There are times when His presence is unbelievably palpable. It's as though someone is watching me from behind. Other times, I'll be walking and sense His presence moving with me. I'm aware of it. It's incredible to know that God may be with you as you go about your daily routine. Now I'd want to ask you a few questions. When you think of the Holy Spirit, what comes to mind? Do you think the Holy Spirit is present when you watch someone quake and fall under the power, or when someone speaks in tongues? Do you refer to a gift of the Spirit as the Holy Spirit when you see it?

So many of us Christians, I'm sure, have misunderstood who the

Holy Spirit is. What you're seeing is the result of the Holy Spirit's work. Who, on the other hand, is the Holy Spirit? I'm not referring to His work as a Counselor or a Teacher. Who is He, exactly? Do you have any idea how He feels? Do you have any idea when He's in pain? Do you understand the Holy Spirit's emotions? How much of God's Spirit's visible presence have you experienced in your life? Consider that for a moment. If you obtain this, it will change your life. I know the Holy Spirit as well as a husband knows his bride. Like a love story, I connect with the Holy Spirit. I am aware of His emotions. I tell Him how much I love Him on a regular basis. Because your relationship with God isn't limited to the Father and Jesus Christ, you can take it to the next level. It's the same with the Holy Spirit. The Father, Son, and Holy Spirit are the three persons that make up God, and if you want to know God fully, you must know all three.

Let's have a look at some texts before we go any farther. Genesis 1:26 And God said, "Let us make man in our image, after our likeness," and "Let them have dominion over the sea creatures, the fowl of the air, the livestock, and all the earth," and "Let them have dominion over every creeping thing that creepeth upon the earth."

Genesis 11:7 Let us go to, let us go down, and there confuse their language so that they don't understand each other.

In the aforementioned texts, the Bible plainly demonstrates that the Father, Son, and Holy Spirit are all working together for a common goal. They all work together, and we need to work together and give each of them our full attention.

As I learned more about the Holy Spirit, I realized that He enjoys it when we begin to acknowledge and respect His presence. Consider how a woman would react if a man she loves said, "I love you." When we say, "Holy Spirit, I want you," he gets excited.

Even if you've said it a hundred times, He enjoys hearing it again and again. When we do, He always shows up in a big way. What is the reason for this? It's because He's warmly greeted, invited, and adored! This brings Him immense joy and enjoyment. Have you ever experienced the Spirit's joy and pleasure? God is so generous and loving, and we must reciprocate. Have you ever felt the Holy Spirit's wrath? There are times when I can tell He is in pain! I've attended numerous sessions, and something bothers Him, and I sense His anguish. When He's sad, I can sense it. I know nothing is said because we're so close.

Ephesians 4:29-32 Allow only excellent speech to come out of your mouth for the sake of edification, so that it may impart grace to those who hear it. And do not grieve God's holy Spirit, by whom you are sealed until the day of redemption. All bitterness, wrath, anger, clamor, and ill speaking, as well as all malice, be put away from you; and be kind to one another, tenderhearted, forgiving one another, even as God has forgiven you for Christ's sake.

Webster's New World Dictionary defines grief as "severe emotional anguish caused by a loss, or the cause of such suffering; to vex."

Do you observe things that irritate the Holy Spirit and things that make Him happy? You can make yourself God's enemy if you talk corrupt, bad words all the time, and if you're always full of bitterness, rage, and clamor. You're in rebellion, and you're grieving the Holy Spirit.

Take a look at this passage from the Book of Isaiah:

Isaiah 63:10 However, they rebelled and irritated his holy Spirit, so he became their enemy and fought against them.

If you make yourself God's enemy, He will fight back, since the Holy Spirit's emotions are something the Father and Jesus are quite protective about. The more time I spend with the Holy Spirit, the more I notice His emotional aspect and wish to shield Him. And He is the one who conveys God's emotions to us, particularly His love. Anyone who speaks a word against the Holy Spirit will be judged by Jesus. To put it another way, who commits blasphemy against the Holy Spirit? The term "blasphemy" refers to the act of speaking in a bad manner.

#988 in Strong's Exhaustive Concordance.

31-32 in Matthew 12 As a result, I say to you, all manner of sin and blasphemy will be forgiven to men, but blasphemy against the Holy Ghost will not be forgiven to mankind. And whoever speaks a word against the Son of Man shall be forgiven; but whoever speaks a word against the Holy Ghost shall not be forgiven, neither in this world nor in the next.

Men will be forgiven every sin and blasphemy against the Son of Man, Jesus, but the Father and Jesus are so protective of the Holy Spirit that blasphemy against Him, speaking against Him, or evil-speaking will not be forgiven. It is an unforgivable sin for which there is no forgiveness. That made me realize that the Holy Spirit requires my undivided attention through a greater closeness.

We require an encounter with the Holy Spirit; we must be in contact with Him, since we can only understand the Holy Spirit's emotions and what pleases Him if we understand His emotions and what pleases Him. 13:14 in 2 Corinthians May the Lord Jesus Christ's grace, God's love, and the Holy Ghost's communion be with you all. Amen.

His remarks are for those of us in the church today who want to have a personal contact with the Holy Spirit. The term "communion" refers to the Holy Spirit's fellowship. So, what does it mean to be in communication with the Holy Spirit? Here's the solution. This type of friendship is based on sharing and unity with the Holy Spirit.

It alludes to involvement, collaboration, close association, and, ultimately, a personal relationship with the Holy Spirit.

Keep in mind that an intimate relationship does not develop quickly. It has progressed. For example, in relation to sharing, I would have fellowship with the Holy Spirit while reading the Bible to Him. He wrote it with the help of men. He should take pleasure in it. After all, it was He who gave birth to the living word! He's a professor, a living professor! I would feel so close to Him when reading Him scripture. I praise Him for all of His promises and begin to put them into practice in my life.

When I didn't understand a passage of Scripture, I would beg Him to explain it to me, and He would. To put it another way, the Holy Spirit and I work together. Every miracle and every healing encourage believers to join together with the Holy Spirit. Yes, God's Spirit is at work, but we have a part to play. What is the depth of your relationship with the Holy Spirit? How strong is your relationship with the Holy Spirit?

You know you can only answer those questions about the bond if you're in the middle of it. I understand how things appear to be handled differently. I want you to understand that the Holy Spirit's person is more than just gifts and manifestations. The Holy Spirit was my primary focus in my search for more of God.

If you skipped over the introduction, you should go back and read it now. My entire walk with God improved as I spent time respecting the Holy Spirit, creating a connection with Him, and growing intimacy.

As I became conscious that the Holy Spirit was vital to everything, I always make every effort to say, "I can't even come into the presence of God without You." I also noted how Christians viewed Him as if He were somewhat inferior to the Father and Jesus Christ, as if He were the body of Christ's servant. We don't believe that according to the Bible, but you'd think we do based on how we treat Him.

During Revivals, Conferences, and even Sundays at Church, we seem to treat the Holy Spirit well, but the problem is that we leave Him there. What about when we're at home alone? What if we say, "Holy Spirit, come to supper"? As Christians, the Holy Spirit has been extremely generous to us. When he attends our sessions, he is filled with joy, rebirth, and regeneration.

Holy Spirit, come!

The fact is that Jesus respected the Holy Spirit, and we must emulate Him. Without the Holy Spirit, he couldn't achieve anything.

Without the Holy Spirit, Jesus would not have been able to enter the world. Mary was overshadowed by the Holy Spirit, who enabled her to conceive the Son of God.

1 Corinthians 1:35 The Holy Ghost will come upon thee, and the power of the Highest will overshadow thee; therefore, that holy thing which shall be born of thee shall be called the Son of God, said the angel.

If Jesus wasn't anointed with the Holy Spirit and given power, He couldn't do anything. Allow yourself to be penetrated by the following scriptures. We are to accomplish the same and even greater things that Jesus did.

3:22 in Luke And the Holy Spirit descended on him in the form of a dove, and a voice from heaven said, Thou are my beloved Son; I am well pleased in thee.

Luke 4:35 And Jesus, full of the Holy Spirit, returned from Jordan and was led into the wilderness by the Spirit, Luke 4:14-21. And Jesus returned to Galilee in the power of the Spirit, and a reputation for him spread throughout the region. He also taught at their synagogues, where he was praised by all. And he returned to Nazareth, his hometown, and, as was his tradition, he entered the synagogue on the Sabbath day and stood up to read. And the book of the prophet Esaias was brought to him. The Spirit of the Lord is upon me because he has anointed me to preach the gospel to the poor; he has sent me to heal the brokenhearted, to preach deliverance to the prisoners, and recovery of sight to the blind, to set at free those who are bruised, to preach the acceptable year of the Lord. He sat down after closing the book and handing it back to the minister.

And all of the people in the synagogue had their gaze fixed on him. And he started speaking to them. This day is the fulfillment of this scripture in your ears.

Acts 10:38 How God anointed Jesus of Nazareth with the Holy Spirit and authority, and how he went about doing good and healing those who were plagued by the demon, since God was with him.

Because Scripture states Jesus gave up His Spirit to the everlasting Spirit, he didn't even die without the Holy Spirit. Without the Holy Spirit, Jesus would not have been able to rise from the grave.

8:11 (Romans) But if you have the Spirit of him who raised Jesus from the dead, he who resurrected Christ from the dead will also revive your mortal bodies by his Spirit who dwells in you.

Amazingly, everything in the Bible revolves around the person of the Holy Spirit, including creation, the outpouring of the Holy Spirit, and miracles. We must devote our entire attention to the Holy Spirit. I'm not referring to the gifts or manifestations, but only for Him.

Everything Jesus Christ did, no matter how wonderful it was, was aided by the Holy Spirit. The Father, Jesus Christ, and the Holy Spirit must all be known. How can we know God in all of his completeness if we don't know all three? There are times in my prayer time when I will focus on Jesus, then feel drawn to God, and then, after a bit, I will focus on the Holy Spirit. With God's visitation and comprehension of the three diverse personalities, this magnificent cycle may persist for hours.

Allow your longing for intimacy with the Holy Spirit to grow stronger. He desires intimacy with you! Allow Him to assist you in taking your relationship to a new level of excitement. Your relationship will continue to grow deeper and deeper if you make intimacy a high priority.

The Holy Spirit's intimacy is nurtured and cultivated. It isn't the result of a fifteen-minute encounter with God. As a result, my goal for this week is to teach you about the Holy Spirit and provide you with a few additional keys to help you grow in closeness with Him.

13:36 John the Baptist Simon Peter asked him, "Lord, where are you going?" Jesus said, "Wherever I go, thou shalt not follow me now," but "then thou shalt follow me."

Listen, your willingness to do what God tells you to do determines the degree to which the Holy Spirit can manifest and intensify in your life. This also demonstrates your love for God by your obedience. So, put obedience to the test!

And I will pray to the Father, and he will send you another Comforter, that he may be with you for ever; even the Spirit of truth; whom the world cannot receive, because it neither sees nor knows him; but ye know him, because he dwells with you and shall be in you.

The world, according to Jesus, cannot receive the Spirit of truth because it does not see or know Him. God said that much of today's church acts like the rest of the world! Many church members have witnessed the Spirit's action, yet they still don't know who He is. There is a significant distinction between seeing and understanding.

We certainly want the Holy Spirit's "with you" presence in our lives now! But are we aware of this existence of unity? Everyone who has been rescued has the presence of the Holy Spirit "in them," but we must know Him if we want to feel and know He is with us, hovering over us in everything we do and wherever we go. It's all about closeness. Then you can't help but feel God's presence in your life through the Holy Spirit.

And what an effect you have on others around you! Examine how the presence of the Holy Spirit impacted individuals through the lives of God's great men and women.

Kathryn Kuhlman had such a powerful presence that when she walked out of her hotel room and passed by, people would be overcome by it. When she went into a kitchen at an event, it was said that the workers felt the presence of the Holy Spirit. She was the Glory's bearer.

Consider the following scenario. The presence of the Holy Spirit in your life is as if Jesus were right there with you in all of His tremendous glory and power.

14:26 (John) But the Comforter, who is the Holy Ghost, whom the Father will send in my name, will teach you everything and bring everything to your mind that I have said to you.

We need the Holy Spirit now more than ever to teach us all truth so that we can overcome the world's falsehood.

Timothy 1:4 Now, the Spirit plainly says that in the last days, some will turn away from the faith, listening to seductive spirits and devilish doctrines.

2 Thessalonians 2:10-11 And with all deceitfulness of unrighteousness in those who perish, because they did not receive the love of the truth, which would save them. God will send them great delusion for this reason, causing them to believe a lie:

As a result, try loving the truth while remaining flexible and teachable. It's a fantastic method to become closer to God's Spirit! What is the Holy Spirit's method for bringing all things to our attention?

The Holy Spirit has the ability to deliver the truth of God's word to our minds. We are conduits for the Holy Spirit's message. For example, I've preached sermons right after receiving revelation. I mean, the revelation will come as I preach. I'm thinking about writing a sermon and going over it again and again. When the time is appropriate, the Holy Spirit will bring things into it. He'll continue to educate me. You are not required to stand in line and wait your turn! All who desire the Holy Spirit will get Him.

4

❧

David, the Psalmist

David is one of the Bible's figures who has had an impact on my life, and I believe we can all learn and grow from him. David was a man who embodied God's character. I understand if you are a man or woman who is solely seeking God and it appears that you are going unnoticed. I want you to know that God, not man, noticed David. For many years, I've witnessed people attempting to be acknowledged by man rather than God. I was one of those that sat back and waited to be discovered, and I can attest to the fact that your gift will find a way to shine.

19:30 Matthew However, many of the first will be the last, and the last will be the first.

Matthew 16:25 For whomever saves his life for my sake will lose it, and whoever loses his life for my cause will find it.

Take a look at this verse:

Isaiah 55:8, 9 is a prophecy from the prophet Isaiah. Because my thoughts are not your thoughts, and your ways are not my ways, declares the LORD. My ways are higher than your ways, and my thoughts are higher than your ideas, just as the skies are higher than the earth.

God desires us to rise higher and walk in deeper spiritual insight and revelation, as you know. Our world doesn't work the same way God does. Many people in this world are obsessed with establishing a good first impression based on their status, reputation, and achievement. Christians are also prone to focusing on this. And it's not that God won't anoint individuals in high positions or who have achieved success.

1:27 Colossians Whom God wishes to reveal the riches of this mystery's glory among the Gentiles, which is Christ in you, the hope of glory:

Listen! God desires to anoint those who appear foolish in the eyes of the world, as well as those who recognize their own weakness and the might of God.

God will not anoint someone because of their age or gender. God wants to anoint us, whether we're young or old, male or female. Regardless of our gender or age, he's ready to use us.

It's critical that everyone has a clear understanding of how much God desires them to embrace the amazing destiny He has prepared for them.

God talked to Jeremiah as a young man about his destiny.

1:5-7 (Jeremiah) I knew thee before I created thee in the womb, and I sanctified thee and anointed thee a prophet to the nations before thou camest forth from the womb. Then I exclaimed, "Ah, Lord GOD!" Because I am a child, I am unable to speak. But the LORD said to me, "Do not say, 'I am a child,' for thou shalt travel to all that I shall send thee, and thou shalt speak whatever I command thee."

Jeremiah was completely trusted by God. He was summoned and selected. God sanctified Jeremiah even before he was born!

The American Heritage Dictionary defines sanctify as "to set apart for religious use; consecrate; render holy; cleanse."

The American Heritage Dictionary defines consecrate as "committed to a sacred aim; sanctified."

When David was an adolescent, God chose him to be Israel's king. Despite the fact that he was the youngest, God chose him. So, what was it about David that drew God's attention?

We need to look at a specific scene immediately before Samuel, the prophet, anointed David as king. When Eliab, one of David's brothers, was brought before Samuel as a probable candidate for king of Israel, the Lord spoke to Samuel, according to Scripture.

16:7 in 1 Samuel But the LORD said to Samuel, "Look not on his countenance, nor on the height of his stature, for I have refused him; for the LORD seeth not as man seeth; for man seeth the external appearance, but the LORD seeth the heart."

God examines the heart of a person.

Eliab appeared to be an excellent match. God, on the other hand, saw his heart. He had knowledge of Eliab's character and thinking life, as well as the ability to see things that no human being could.

16:10 in 1 Samuel Jesse made seven of his sons pass before Samuel once more. The LORD hath not chosen these, Samuel said to Jesse.

In the eyes of his family, David was probably just another sheepherder, but God saw things differently. He could see what no one else could: what was going on inside David. David, for example, loved God and worshipped Him in spirit and truth while taking his job seriously caring to the sheep. And God admired his bravery as he fought off lions and other predators who sought to eat the family's herd. But God was looking; He was taking notice!

Samuel must have been perplexed when he discovered that six of Jesse's sons were not acceptable to the Lord.

16:11 in 1 Samuel And Samuel asked Jesse, "Are all thy children here?" And he added, "There is still the youngest, and look, he keeps the sheep." And Samuel replied to Jesse, "Send and collect him," since we won't sit down until he arrives.

"Samuel was not influenced by his family's thinking!" Within seconds, Samuel saw in his spirit that this young guy was God's chosen one.

"Arise, anoint him; because he is the one!" Samuel heard God say. It didn't matter that David was the youngest and was not well-liked by his family on the surface. His heart was so attractive to God on the inside.

From the moment Samuel anointed him with oil, the Lord's Spirit descended upon him. Because of his close relationship with God, I believe the Holy Spirit couldn't help but pour out on him from that day forward! David had never grieved the Holy Spirit, so the Holy Spirit couldn't wait to come on him!

That's the one He frequently chooses, even if it appears to be weak and silly. God doesn't simply want to reach out to the youth; He wants to raise them up to preach the gospel with anointing and anoint them for kingship.

The remainder of the story is excellent as well, but I'd like to focus on a little portion of it. Above everything else, David was chosen. He could entertain the King with music. He was promoted several times. Being King wasn't easy, but it was a process.

Because of his heartfelt devotion to God, God's favor was bestowed upon him. David's family reacted furiously when God blessed him with an increase. The one who accuses the brethren! He was undeterred by his brother's claims.

I want you to understand that when your heart is right before the Lord, you can do things you never thought possible. The giant was slain by David. David was in the midst of a spiritual conflict. There's something to be said for someone who knows the living God and doesn't get angry when they're insulted!

16:32 (Proverbs) He who is slow to anger is better than the powerful, and he who rules his spirit is better than he who conquers a city.

We've all been on the receiving end of erroneous assessments. Like David's brother, it's sometimes the people closest to you who make the most alarming charges. That is a lesson that we all need to learn. But, do you know what God has to say about it?

54:17 in Isaiah No weapon created against thee shall prosper, and thou shalt condemn every voice that rises against thee in judgment. This is the LORD's servants' inheritance, and their righteousness is mine, says the LORD.

Take a look at 1 Samuel 17:33. And Saul said to David, "Thou art not able to battle with this Philistine; for thou art a youth, and he hath been a man of war from his youth."

David's response was fantastic.

1 Samuel 17:34–36 And David answered to Saul, "Thy servant watched his father's sheep, and there came a lion and a bear and snatched a lamb out of the flock; and I went out after him, smote him, and delivered it out of his mouth; and when he arose against me, I grasped him by his beard, and hit him, and slaughtered him." Because he opposed the armies of the living God, thy servant murdered both the lion and the bear, and this uncircumcised Philistine shall be as one of them.

When Goliath spotted David approaching, he assessed him, took note of his youth, and began hurling insults, curses, and death threats at him, but David was unfazed. He was aware of His Creator. He held firm and, guided by God, issued a judgment against his foe that greatly surpassed the giant's boastful death threats.

Then David addressed the Philistine, saying, "Thou comest to me with a sword, a spear, and a shield; but I come to thee in the name of the LORD of hosts, the God of Israel's armies, whom thou hast defied." The LORD will deliver thee into my hand this day, and I will smite thee and remove thy head from thee; and I will give the carcasses of the Philistine army to the fowls of the air and the wild beasts of the land this day, that all the earth may know that there is a God in Israel.

David released his stone with a single strike, and Goliath fell. God is seeking for people who will not be intimidated by the land's "giants." What are the modern-day giants? There is religion, tradition, apathy, abortion, and claiming to be religious yet denying God's power.

3:5 (2 Timothy) Turn away from those who have a form of godliness but deny its power.

God is looking for people who can be used by Him, people who are devoted lovers of God with a passionate heart, a God-seeking heart like David's.

He's looking for "Davids" who are willing to entirely devote their lives to Him and allow Him to hone their spiritual muscles in the trenches. To further His kingdom, God will bring us together with like-minded others.

So don't get discouraged if you aren't valued or recognized, or if you are frequently overlooked.

When you love God with all your heart, like David did, or as you wish to be today, God can easily keep you moving forward, one step at a time, according to His plan. Encourage one another. David took one step at a time, following God's lead. It's the same way with your God-ordained destiny: it's a step-by-step procedure. Consider how David began his ascension to the throne. It's pretty amazing! He rose from a shepherd to become the King of Israel.

5

Worshipper's Fragrance

When we worship with a pure heart, we emit a fragrance to the Lord. I invite the Holy Spirit to come over you and hover.

60:13 Isaiah The fir tree, pine tree, and box combined will bring the beauty of Lebanon to thee, to adorn the place of my sanctuary; and I will make the place of my feet gorgeous.

If we are to touch the very heart of Jesus Christ, we must be filled with passion, praise, adoration, and closeness. These are words that must affect the center of our existence. We will experience God's presence among us when we are a church of passionate individuals filled with new love who seek the Lord's presence. And anything can happen when the Lord's presence comes upon us: deliverance, healing, restoration, forgiveness, and cleaning. However, believers frequently fight with God, feeling stuck, and attempting to persuade Him to meet their needs rather than just contacting Him and enjoying His presence.

I'd like to question how we live and relate to Jesus Christ, as well as our loving relationship with Him. I'm going to ask you how much of a Jesus follower you are.

6–13 in Matthew 26 When Jesus was in Bethany, at Simon the leper's house, a lady with an alabaster box of extremely costly ointment came up to him and poured it on his head as he sat at dinner. When his followers saw it, however, they were outraged, asking, "To what use is this waste?" Because of this, the ointment may have been sold for a high price and donated to the needy. When Jesus realized what was going on, he asked them, "Why are you bothering the woman?" She has done a terrific work in my life. Because you always have the poor with you, but you don't always have me. She performed it for my burial in that she poured this ointment on my body. Indeed, I say unto you, wherever this gospel is spread throughout the world, this woman's deed will be told as a monument to her.

This was the description of a woman who came to Jesus with an alabaster bottle of perfume and anointed His head and feet. When I read these two verses, what struck me the most was when the Holy Spirit showed that the anointing of Bethany isn't just about anointing Jesus for His burial and resurrection. This actual narrative, on the other hand, can teach us how to be abandoned lovers of Jesus if our hearts are open.

She was inspired with such zeal for Jesus that she was able to face and defy all of the established rules. She pushed past her dignity and any concerns about what others would think of her. Mary's love for Jesus was so strong that nothing could deter her from approaching her Master's feet.

Mary offered Jesus her whole attention and affection when her sister, Martha, welcomed Him into their home, according to the Bible.

Take a look at this. Luke 10:38-40 is a parallel scripture to this narrative. As they traveled, he got to a certain village, where he was welcomed into the home of a certain woman named Martha. She also had a sister named Mary, who sat at Jesus' feet and listened to his words. But Martha, tired of serving so much, approached him and said, Lord, dost thou not notice that my sister has left me to serve alone? As a result, I implore her to assist me.

Mary was unconcerned about all the things that needed to be done, and she resisted the urge to get busy because she was content with only one thing she could do for God: being close to Him, looking into His eyes and hearing His voice.

We will deliver better worship if we become more impassioned. Do you know why Mary was such a passionate woman? It was because Mary realized she had been saved from a pit of spiritual darkness. She recalled what it was like to live a life without God. Because of her deep love and dedication to Jesus, I believe she went to the Pharisee's house to see Him. I suppose she was unaware of the prophetic meaning of anointing Jesus for burial. Rather, her entire motivation stemmed from a passionate love for her King, and her appreciation and respect for Jesus drew her to His side. God wants us to have the same passionate love for Him in our hearts.

How can we rekindle our enthusiasm now? One way is to never forget the pit of darkness from which Jesus rescued us due to His immense mercy and love for us.

(Luke 7:40-42). And Jesus responded by saying, Simon, I have something to say to thee. And he says, "Master, go ahead." There was a creditor who had two debtors: one owed 500 pence and the other 50. And when they couldn't afford to pay, he pardoned them both. So, one of them do you think will love him the most?

We can see that Jesus was comparing Simon's and Mary's passions here. Simon didn't believe he needed to be forgiven because he was a Pharisee and a holy man. I feel that we all need to rediscover our passion so that we can admit that we have all been sinners. We are all sinners, according to the Bible. Because I know what Jesus has done in my own life, I know how it changed my worship. Unfortunately, many people in the church today have forgotten their responsibility to Jesus. They've forgotten about the hole from which God rescued them. As's why they don't have the same passion or fire for Jesus that they did when they were first rescued and He was their first love. Here's an example of a man who doesn't understand emotion, admiration, devotion, or thankfulness because he puts his faith in his religion. He asked Jesus, "Do you not realize what kind of woman this is?" with his spiritual ego intact.

7:37 in Luke When a sinful woman in the city learned that Jesus was eating dinner at the Pharisee's house, she brought an alabaster bottle of ointment.

The scented oil, on the other hand, is pricey and reserved for rare occasions. It was so expensive that it would have cost at least a year's earnings now. But no price would be spared for Mary; her deep love for Jesus could only be shown by pouring out all of her most valuable and costly possessions on Him. In addition, Mary's dedication required her to break open her alabaster box in order for the fragrant oil to stream out, a symbol of her brokenness before the Lord. We can perceive Mary's emotions as she cleaned Jesus' feet with her hair; impassioned sobbing, her tears dripping with the holy oil. How close was the scent of aromatic oil that lingered in the air to you?

What occurred next, and it's the same thing that happens in a lot of churches today when someone worships with zeal?

The next step was criticism.

8 and 9 in Matthew 26 When his followers saw it, however, they were outraged, asking, "To what use is this waste?" Because of this, the ointment may have been sold for a high price and donated to the needy.

Jesus is worth everything I have and am, which is why I gave Him everything. Mary's attitude was like this.

We must worship like Mary did if we are to truly touch God's heart with our worship; we must treasure this form of worship. What I want us to focus on is how Mary's worship left such an indelible impact on God's heart that He said.

26:13 in Matthew Indeed, I say unto you, wherever this gospel is spread throughout the world, this woman's deed will be told as a monument to her.

Now, I'd like to pose a question to us. Is it possible that our worship and love to Jesus has such an impact on God's heart that it continues to bless the angels and God even after all these years?

Are they still reminiscing about the time we touched Him?

Is God even aware of the manner in which we worship? I believe that in worshiping God, there is a place of such intimacy and abandonment that we can touch Him to the point of scaring Him.

8:6 in Song of Songs Set me as a seal on thy heart, as a seal on thy arm: for love is as strong as death; jealousy is as terrible as the tomb; the coals thereof are coals of fire, with a ferocious flame.

If our worship does not unleash all of who we are and does not cost us everything, it isn't authentic worship.

Our hearts are like the alabaster box carrying priceless jewels drenched in perfume. However, we must allow the Holy Spirit to crush our hearts in His own unique way. He fractures our hearts for a reason, so we can give God our truly fragrant adoration. Brokenness allows us to die to ourselves and our inhibitions, allowing us to worship God with enormous enthusiasm and freedom.

We can even follow in the footsteps of Moses! When he descended the mountain after 40 days of being in the Lord's glory, he didn't even notice His face shone with the brilliance of God's glory.

34:29 (Exodus) And it came to pass that when Moses descended from Mount Sinai with the two tables of testimony in his hand, Moses was unaware that the skin of his face shined while he conversed with him.

In the midst of the Glory, Moses lost sight of himself.

Christians, too, are a part of the priesthood today. 1 Peter 2:9 says that we are a chosen generation. But you are a chosen generation, a royal priesthood, a holy nation, a peculiar people, that ye should shew forth the praises of him who hath called you out of darkness into his marvelous light: When we fail to worship God with everything within us, our body, soul, and spirit, and only draw close to God with our lips, we've taken the sweetness out of our incense of worship.

When we lose our passion for our first love, Jesus, and don't have a burning heart for Him, the perfume that has the potential to remain in heaven long after we've touched His heart is absent! The purity of the incense in our worship is tainted when we fail to hold God's holiness in high respect. God desires a sweet aroma to fill His nostrils, and He seeks pure incense in our worship, but how will we grab His attention if it isn't manifesting?

2:2 (Leviticus) And he shall bring it to Aaron's sons, the priests, and he shall take his handful of flour, oil, and frankincense from it, and the priest shall burn the remembrance of it thereon the altar, to be a sacrifice made by fire, of a sweet savour unto the LORD:

God does not want believers to be content with merely attending scheduled services and singing the same hymns all of the time.

You know, at church, we can sing and converse with a buddy at the same time, with a dash of carnality thrown in. We've also removed some of God's Sweet Smell from our worship since we don't even press in.

We mix in lethargy and disinterest if the entertainment of worship isn't there for us to grab hold of. When we give the Lord all of ourselves, on the other hand, we heighten the beautiful aroma of the perfume in our worship. I've been to some of the driest religious worship services, but I resolved in my heart to worship God with everything I had: body, mind, soul, strength, and emotions completely engaged. Also, the pleasant smell of the incense is heightened in our worship when we take leadership over our worry about those around us and let the creative passion of love for God to emerge inside of us. When we dance in front of the Lord's presence, the perfume of our worship pleases Him. Even if we are unable to physically dance before the Lord, we can dance in our minds, which thrills the Lord and adds to the richness of our worship.

True adoration to Jesus occurs when we become so engrossed in the presence of the Lord that we lose track of everything else. Any barricades that attempted to keep us out of the Holy of Holies were pushed aside.

We forget about everything, just as David did, and surrender everything we have to the Lord in worship.

6:14 in 2 Samuel David was girded with a linen ephod and danced before the LORD with all his might.

4:24 (John) Because God is a Spirit, those who worship him must do so in spirit and truth.

Also, we don't want to offend God by failing to make changes in the areas of our life where He is calling us to do so. Sin stinks when we worship any secret. I'm not suggesting we don't make mistakes. But we can only be right with God because of His kindness and mercy. We must deal with issues such as forgiveness and locations where we know God is working. Deception will ensue if we push our sin down, and we don't want that in our worship of God.

We want to be worshippers who obey God. Trying to glorify God while walking in disobedience never works. Our disobedience deprives God of the pleasure He would have gotten if we had obeyed Him.

15:22 in 1 Samuel And Samuel said, "Does the LORD take as much pleasure in burnt offerings and sacrifices as in obeying the LORD's voice?" Listening is better than sacrifice, and obeying is better than ram fat.

Obeying the Lord makes us feel clean and generates a lovely aroma in our worship that He enjoys.

Many believers seek to glorify Jesus by worshiping Him in a way that will leave a mark or scar on His heart, so that He will remember the day they touched His heart with their worship for the rest of His life. I want to wear a scent, a perfume, and have an aroma that stays in the air long after I've finished worshiping. When we worship Jesus in spirit and truth, we honor Him. He is deserving of recognition!

6

⚜

Make contact with God

What did Jesus say to Lazarus, who had been dead in the tomb for four days? Did I not tell you that if you believe, you will see God's glory? he asked.

According to Jesus' statement, what is God's glory? It's humans who have been resurrected from the dead. It's the Glory's resurrection power at work.

Do you consider the Bible to be true from beginning to end? Do you believe Jesus is the same now as He was yesterday, and that He will be the same in the future? What a wonderful opportunity for healing we have. What about the unexplainable? Why can't He visit me like He visited Abraham, Daniel, Isaiah, John, and Ezekiel if He is the same today? Jesus is the same today as He was yesterday, and He will be forever, thus everything in the Bible is still relevant today. There are supernatural encounters as well as healing and laying hands on the ill. Jesus was raised from the grave and lived in His resurrected form for forty days. If He is still alive now, supernatural events may occur. In a visitation, Jesus can appear to someone.

My eyes started to open a few years ago, and I began to see angels. Angels appearing and speaking to Mary and Joseph appear to be acceptable, but angels speaking to us do not. We don't mind if Paul is brought to the "third heaven," as he called it. Paul and Elijah were ordinary men, just like us. God must have a supernatural interaction with someone. He's the same today as he was then.

Why should Christianity and Christian experiences be any different today than they were in the Bible?

"It is his angel," they remarked as Peter turned up at the door after an all-night prayer group. They didn't want to think Peter was present, but they were willing to believe it was his angel. They had been praying for Peter's release from prison, but when he arrived at the door, they didn't recognize him.

We will hear stories of larger interactions and experiences as God pours out His greater majesty. They will be based on how God seemed to people in the Bible.

I've had some weird encounters. I'm finally feeling free to talk about some of those things. This year, Jesus appeared to me twice. I've had moments when God's presence was so intense that I could hear and feel electric waves. I would move my arms and hear woooooo sounds. (This is the best sound I can think of for typing.) I lift my head and woooooo, then lift my other arm, and the sound repeats itself. It was as though an electric power had come from God's heavenly domain. Are you prepared to meet God? This is a straightforward visitation. I want you to know that visitations do happen. Why do we need biblical encounters when we have the Bible, argues religion?

It's all about closeness. What's the point in waiting for your inheritance? What do you want to find when you get in heaven? God's kingdom is near; it resides within you. Now I'm starving. I am a joint heir to the estate. Thank God, the fullness will come one day, and I will be in paradise, but I do not have to wait for my inheritance until then.

We need to have more faith and hope that He will talk to us and come to see us. Heaven is a real, palpable place. Heaven's glory is real, and it transforms everything it touches. I see a window that appears to be open, and I can glimpse into heaven. Heaven, on the other hand, has come from the Lord. God once told me that Heaven is more interested in being discovered than we are in discovering it.

I saw a massive golden door in my vision. It had a keyhole, and I held the key in my hand. (Prior to this vision, I heard a Word from the Lord saying that God was giving me the master key.) When I opened the door, I was greeted by something more lovely than words can describe.

In this vision, I was accompanied by a number of folks. I looked around and saw valuables aplenty, including jewels, gold, and jewelry. All of this happened before the signs and marvels began to appear at my meetings. It was quite bright in that chamber, and as I moved my gaze ahead, the light became even brighter. I noticed a pair of sandal-clad feet. I could see that they were sitting on a throne after peering closer, and the presence of God washed over me at that same instant. God was seated on His throne. I heard Him say, "Come in; there is enough place for everyone." He invited us to join Him on His throne. I saw the throne room during my event. WOW!

I heard several voices singing one song with many words at the same time during another visitation. It was like a concert or an angel choir. "You are good, you are fantastic, you are beautiful, and you are lovely," they kept repeating. It was a song that validated my worthiness. (In God's eyes) It felt as though the Father was singing with joy over me. They broke through rejection, fear, and other barriers, and the beams radiated the Father's love.

23:1-6 (Psalms) A Davidic psalm. I will not go hungry because the

LORD is my shepherd. He leads me beside quiet waters and makes me lie down in green pastures. For the sake of his name, he restores my soul and leads me down the ways of righteousness. I will not be afraid even if I walk through the valley of the shadow of death, for thou art with me, and thy rod and staff comfort me. In the midst of my foes, you set a banquet for me; you anoint my head with oil, and my cup overflows. Surely goodness and mercy will be with me throughout the days of my life, and I will live in the LORD's home forever.

Revelations 2:7 Let him who has an ear hear what the Spirit says to the churches; and to him who overcometh, I will give to eat of the tree of life, which is in the midst of God's paradise.

Let anybody who has an ear hear what the Spirit has to say to the churches. I will give the right to eat from the tree of life, which is in God's paradise, to whoever overcomes. I'm sharing this because I'd like to bring heaven closer to earth. When the Lord appears, anything can happen. We desire greater levels of glory than we already possess. We would eat the fruit of the Tree of Life, according to the Lord's promise. I pray that you will be willing to step into a new dimension of glory. Allow the heavens to open their doors!

I was planning to end this chapter here, but I feel compelled to write down what God has just said to me. I'd like to write about miracles, signs, and wonders.

Miracles, Signs, and Wonders

We are on the verge of a profound spiritual awakening in which signs, wonders, and miracles will become the norm. In addition, we will discover the supernatural, which will become natural, the ordinary, which will become remarkable, and the impossible, which will become feasible, in every condition and at all times! We are witnessing a worldwide awakening and demonstration of the Holy Spirit's power and supernatural deeds by those who have been touched by God and are living for Him.

2 Timothy 2:17-19 And it shall come to pass, says God, that in the latter days I will pour out my Spirit on all flesh: Your sons and daughters will prophesy, your young men will see visions, and your elderly people will dream dreams: In those days, I will pour out my Spirit on my servants and handmaidens, and they will prophesy: And I will show signs in the sky above and wonders on the ground below; blood, fire, and mist of smoke:

Matthew 10:7–8 And wherever you go, preach, proclaiming that the kingdom of heaven is near. Freely ye have received, freely give: heal the sick, cleanse the lepers, raise the dead, cast out devils.

God's healing anointing is sweeping the land, revival winds are blowing, and God's people are ablaze for Him!

Mark 16:20 And they went out and preached everywhere, with the Lord assisting them and confirming the message with signs. Amen.

John 4:48 Then Jesus answered to him, "You will not believe unless you see signs and wonders."

20:30, 31 are two verses in John's gospel. And Jesus performed many additional signs in the presence of his followers that are not recorded in this book: These are written, however, in order for you to believe that Jesus is the Christ, the Son of God, and that by believing you may have life through his name.

In my ministry, God has performed numerous signs and miracles. I spoke at a revival in Litchfield, Illinois. Thousands of gemstones and pounds of glory dust were found. Many individuals are skeptical after seeing gemstones arrive in large piles. The Church is the only thing standing in the way of the Church. That's right, you read it accurately. All of us are criticizing and pulling down our Christian brothers and sisters. This revival lasted two years and featured a powerful presence of God as well as numerous manifestations.

The critics who arrived were the same folks who said how amazing the signs and miracles were. I want you to understand that uncertainty is a spirit that takes possession of a person. So many signs were found in people's purses, Bibles, clothing, homes, cars, and other places. God's gold fillings were numerous. I want you to realize that there will be critics when you open God's Glory like we did. That will be covered in a later chapter.

I'd want to wrap up this chapter by sharing some recent testimonials. These testimonies took place following a meeting.

(For the sake of anonymity, the names of those involved have been changed.)

This is what a husband said about his wife: "Oh, no! My wife was cleaning her teeth Sunday evening after last weekend's sessions in Springfield when she saw all of her fillings [approximately ten] had changed to gold! After the meetings, she was on fire and anointed. That she even gave a fantastic sermon on Sunday morning! All honor and glory to Yeshua the Messiah!"

Bill, after hearing your anointed message on Saturday night and discerning that YOU ARE A LEADER OF THIS ILLINOIS REVIVAL, as well as the accuracy of your WORDS OF KNOWLEDGE TO THOSE I WAS WITH, AND MYSELF FOR, AT LEAST, A 1/2 HOUR INTERMITTENTLY ABOUT LITERATURE, WRITING BOOKS AND BOOKLETS, without getting you puffed up, I will say now that

A guy who has attended many meetings testified, "During praise and worship yesterday, I looked down and noticed a jewel at my feet." God is wonderful!! (This is what he said on Sunday morning at his church.)

A woman who has been attending my sessions has given the following testimony: Hello, Bill.

I was unable to attend the meetings this past weekend, but I wanted to let you know that last night I discovered a gorgeous gemstone in my home. It appeared on the floor of my bathroom. I had dropped a shirt on the floor, and when I bent down to pick it up, it was there next to the shirt, maybe 5 minutes later. It's just stunning! God be praised! You mentioned God doing some incredible things in our home, and you weren't joking! God is a good God. The diamond in our home, I believe, is a sign that the Lord is doing incredible things in our family, both physically and spiritually!

A woman who has been to the majority of my meetings, Greetings, Bill My kid and I both have gold dust on our faces, which has turned various hues. On the right side of my neck, I have some. We are both surprised and astonished. I'm not shocked because I've sensed His presence in and around my home. I've also been blasting your CD in the house where all of this is taking place, with the diamond appearing and glory dust on our faces. It occurs in the bathroom as we prepare to retire for the night.

God be praised.

Aren't they fantastic? People will speak ill of you and even attempt to demolish what God is doing in the process. No one is going to be able to stop God from manifesting His magnificent goodness and amazing signs and wonders.

Getting Ready for His Arrival

It boggles my mind that God has made the intellect of Christ available to us, the manifestation of truth, humility, righteousness, holiness, meekness, wisdom, and understanding. This is truly what is being provided to us by His Holy Spirit, the invitation to be one with Him who is one with the Father, even to the point of living life with Christ's mind.

Revelation 2:16 Who knows the thoughts of the Lord to be able to counsel him? We, on the other hand, have Christ's thinking.

Though unimaginable to contemplate, it was made possible by His grace and the Holy Spirit. There is, however, one snag. That is the process of dying every day until it is Christ who lives in me and not I who lives.

15:31 in 1 Corinthians I die every day because of your joy, which I enjoy in Christ Jesus our Lord.

Thank God, we can only attain the mind of Christ through this procedure. Otherwise, a lot of dangerous people would be running about with God's thoughts, exploiting them to further their own goals. We must train our thoughts to think in terms of the Kingdom. This is how Jesus presented it to the disciples as the way to live this life. In Matthew, just as the crowds get large and "His fame spread across Syria," Jesus walks to the top of the mountain, sits, and waits for the disciples to come to Him before speaking. We should all take precautions in the coming days as He unleashes power and authority that the earth has never seen before.

3-5 Matthew 5: The poor in spirit are blessed, for theirs is the kingdom of heaven. Blessed are those who weep, for they will be consoled. The meek are blessed, since they will inherit the earth.

The word meek denotes "humbled by sorrow" in this context. I don't know many folks who aren't suffering from or have recently suffered from some ailment. When properly walked through, it does, in fact, develop character. There will come a time when everything in this physical realm will be under our control. Some will reach a point of oneness with God where they can say, "Mountain be moved," and it will happen. Others will not be bound by the laws or constraints of the physical realm, and will stroll out onto the water and over it for the Kingdom's job, not for some spectacular spectacle. Many will be translated from one location to another. As we die to self, serve others, and become one with Him as we dedicate ourselves to this death process, it will be inconceivable. It will become simpler to die to oneself. Count your blessings! This is the fate of the current generation! In and through God, this is your destiny!

1 & 3 James Count it all joy, my friends, when ye are tempted in many ways, knowing that the testing of your faith produces patience.

We must persevere and overcome the difficulties. We must also overcome the need to be acknowledged and praised for what we have accomplished, despite the fact that it is only what the Lord allows us to participate in as He works through us. Above all, we are instructed to not only embrace and move through it in love and death to self, but also to be grateful for it!

5:15-18 in 1 Thessalonians Make sure that no one repays ill for evil, and that you always do what is right, both among yourselves and to others. Continue to rejoice. Continue to pray without ceasing. Give thanks under all circumstances, because this is God's wish for you in Christ Jesus.

I know we've all heard it and know it in our heads, but walking it out is a different story. We must encourage one another so that as many people as possible will conquer and become God's earthly buddies! The most valuable aspect of all of this is being a friend of God. He reveals his secrets to his pals, those who will take up His cross and follow Him even through Christ's sufferings. We need to develop into someone He can trust with these secrets, people who will not reveal them unless he releases us. When He tells us something or offers us experience in Him, He must be able to trust us. If you tell a friend a secret and they tell others, you realize that you can't trust them and stop sharing personal information with them.

20:19 (Proverbs) Meddle not with him who flattereth with his lips, for he who goes about like a talebearer reveals secrets.

The idea is that God is looking for people to whom He may entrust incredible things in the coming days, more so than at any previous moment in history. We are ecstatic about it, but we prefer to ignore the fact that there is a cost. We must be people who have truly died to themselves, who seek God in prayer and friendship, and who can be trusted not to tell everyone everything we know. According to Jesus, He only did what He witnessed the Father do. He just said what He was told to say by the Father. That doesn't mean He understood everything or could have done everything; it only means He was obedient and could be trusted to act only when His Father commanded Him to. Is it possible to get by with anything less than the very Son of God? Oh, to be a God's buddy! That kind of intimacy with our heavenly Father is something I adore. With Him, all else will flow out of that place. The cost of preparing ourselves for His presence is high, but the benefits are immeasurable. These are the ones that are referred to as God's buddies!

7

Habitation Preparation

I'd like to expand on what God is doing by laying out some options for creating a sanctuary that is welcoming to the Holy Spirit.

Isaiah 66:1 "The heaven is my throne, and the earth is my footstool," declares the LORD. "Where is the house that men build for me?" And where will I be able to rest?

We must learn how to build God a sanctuary, modify the furnishings, and pursue the ark of God safely if we are to be ready for the abode of God.

God gave Moses a pattern for the tabernacle and all its furnishings when He needed a place to dwell among the Israelites:

Exodus 25:8, 9 is a passage from the book of Exodus. And let them build a sanctuary for me so that I might live among them. You shall make it according to all that I show thee, following the pattern of the tabernacle, and the pattern of all its instruments.

God is a perfectionist when it comes to order and design. He desires to manifest what is in His mind through us! We're largely ministering to His heart when we grow to understand and carry out what He desires in both the spiritual and natural spheres. It's as if we're ministering to God Himself! The first thing we must understand about constructing a sanctuary is that we cannot construct one for God without also constructing one for ourselves, because both sanctuaries are intertwined. We need to create a space in our hearts and a real location where God can come and stay.

If we welcome someone to stay with us, we make sure they have a place to stay. What makes you think God is any different? We need a sacred space, a place set apart for meeting with God, where the Holy Spirit is invited to reside in the atmosphere of our hearts, homes, and churches.

Do you have a certain area in your home that you consider sacred? Is it even possible for you to meet with God? Is there a time in your life when you've made it a priority to go to the secret place of the Most High and stay there? The first requirement for constructing a sanctuary is that we must have a strong desire to construct God's dwelling.

We must be starving and desperate. It all begins with a desire. Every day, I've created a resting space in my life via prayer and communication with Him. When no one is looking, I spend my days and nights focusing on God's Word. I require a sacred space where I may go alone and commune with God. I'm looking for a place to live.

Is there a spot where you may wait in the splendor during your devotional time? You will never have a habitation if you do not have a sanctuary and a sacred place in your daily life and in your church that extends beyond gatherings at conferences and churches. There will be visitors. God will appear, and you will have an encounter with Him, but He will never stay because He prefers to rest in places where people have made a place for him to rest. Do you know how a church prepares a sanctuary and makes it ready for God to live there? It happens when we establish an environment conducive to the Holy Spirit by keeping the church open for prayer, supplication, and seeking God's face in addition to conferences and revival meetings. There should be a prayer area in the church that is open twenty-four hours a day, seven days a week. There must be a gathering place for the church to come together and seek God. When there is revival, the prayer room opens and the intercessors gather an hour before the service, but where are they the rest of the week?

It will cost us money and put a strain on our resources. But how much do we really desire God? We want God's presence to linger from one day to the next when He comes and pours out His glory, so we set apart an atmosphere, a sacred location, and a sanctuary for Him to stay and dwell with us.

So, while we're not there, I'd like to urge us to leave praise music playing in our homes and churches 24 hours a day, because the worship will continue to effect the atmosphere while it's playing. We don't only want God's visitation; we want Him to live with us, so we need a space where we can listen to worship music and concentrate on the Bible. We need a location where we can not only cry out to God, but also where we can return to an open heaven. There is still a well of God's glory residing in heaven that we can re-open in any place where there has ever been a revival. It was never supposed to be closed in the first place!

Let me paint a picture of habitation for you based on Noah's life. The floodwaters came and swamped the earth after he built the ark. This is God's wrath (Gen. 6 & 7).

8:8, 9 in Genesis He also sent out a dove to see if the waters had receded from the face of the ground; but the dove found no rest for the sole of her foot, and she returned to him into the ark, because the waters were still on the face of the whole earth; so he put out his hand and took her, and drew her in unto him into the ark.

Do you know how to draw the Holy Spirit to yourself?

Genesis 8:10, 11 are two of the most important verses in the

Bible. And he stayed another seven days, and then he sent the dove out of the ark again; and the dove came in to him in the evening, and there, in her mouth was an olive leaf plucked off: so Noah knew the waters had subsided. The dove with the olive leaf in its mouth represents the anointing of the Holy Spirit upon us. The Holy Spirit will come to rest on us when we live in a way that invites Him in. The Spirit of God will rest on us when we have a hidden place and time set out for meeting with God when no one is looking. When we construct a spiritual tabernacle, He will rest on us. God is following in Noah's footsteps! He's sending out His dove, the Holy Spirit, and the ultimate desire of His heart as He pours out His Spirit is for the dove to find a place to rest her soul. However, we frequently get merely a visitation when the dove arrives since our lifestyle does not provide a safe haven for His presence. As a result, the dove flees, and God must send out another dove to see whether anyone wishes for Him to dwell and stay with them.

The Spirit of God is looking for a place to rest His feet, and He's looking for people who are so devoted to His Word, prayer, and keeping the heavens open that He feels driven to live with them.

When we work together with the Holy Spirit to create an atmosphere that pleases Him, we call it open heaven. This aura will pervade the sanctuary we're constructing, but why are we constructing a sanctuary in the first place? What are we trying to achieve? Why do we desire God to live among us?

Do you recall David's desire to build a house for God in his heart?

7:1–13 in 2 Samuel When the king sat in his house, and the LORD had granted him respite from all his adversaries around him, the king said to Nathan the prophet, "See now, I dwell in a cedar house, but the ark of God dwelleth within curtains." And Nathan answered to the king, "Go, do whatever your heart desires; for the LORD is with you." The word of the LORD came to Nathan that night, saying, "Go and tell my servant David, Thus saith the LORD,

Shalt thou build me a house for me to reside in?" Whereas, from the time I took the children of Israel out of Egypt until now, I have walked in a tent and a tabernacle. I spoke a word with any of the tribes of Israel whom I commanded to feed my people Israel in all the areas where I went with all the children of Israel, saying, Why build ye not me a home of cedar? So thou shalt say to my servant David, Thus saith the LORD of hosts, I took thee from the sheepcote, from following the sheep, to be ruler over my people, over Israel: And I was with thee wherever thou wentest, and have cut off all thine enemies from thy sight, and have given thee a great name, like the names of the great men of the earth. Furthermore, I will appoint a place for my people Israel, and I will plant them, so that they may dwell in a place of their own and no longer move; nor shall the children of wickedness afflict them, as they have done in the past, and since the time that I commanded judges to be over my people Israel, and have delivered thee from all thy enemies. Also, the LORD says that he will build you a house. And when thy days are done, and thou sleepest with thy fathers, I will raise up thy seed after thee, who will come forth from thy bowels, and I will establish his reign. I will establish the throne of his kingdom for all time if he builds a house for my name.

Solomon, his son, completed the duty of constructing God's home. Solomon addressed the people after the building program was completed and the Ark of the Covenant was brought inside the temple.

1 Kings 8:17-19 is a passage from the book of 1 Kings. And it was in David's father's heart to construct a home in the name of the LORD God of Israel. Whereas it was in thine heart to build a house for my name, thou didst well that it was in thine heart, the LORD declared to David my father. Nonetheless, thou shalt not construct the house; rather, thy son who shall be born of thy loins shall construct the building in my name.

That was not just his heart's desire, but also his father, David's. Their intentions were sincere. Many people desire God's presence to arrive, and they want to construct Him a refuge, but their motivations aren't pure. Some people desire God because of the benefits it will bring to their church or speaking engagements. Others want God to come and bring a revival to their church so that their finances will increase or they will be recognized. This is not to say that God does not want to come and pour out all of His blessings. God, on the other hand, is seeking for people who desire to build a space and create an atmosphere where the Holy Spirit is welcome, not just say the proper words.

Do we desire for God to reside in our midst in the same manner that David desired for God to dwell in his midst because he had a burning desire for God?

Or are we only interested in what God has done for us?

What's going on with God in your secret place?

Do you have a place where you can go to get away from it all? Is there a time in your schedule set aside for you to meet with God, or do you wait until the next round of meetings?

In my life, I've learned that if there's no pool in the desert, I'll find an underground spring if I dig deep enough. In my refuge, I have a well. I've instilled a desire, as well as an atmosphere and a way of life, that embraces God. He wishes to stay!

The term "dwell" means "to stay; to abide; to reside; to settle down."

When God comes to us, He wants to make a home with us. It does not imply that when God appears, we will have an encounter. That isn't a place to live.

God appearing at revival meetings is not a habitation; a habitation occurs when the Lord's presence remains in the building or lingers on your flesh. It's the scent, the fragrance of Christ. Even if you don't say anything, the fragrance of Christ emanates from you, and people exclaim, "You've been with Jesus!"

God is aware of the churches and individuals who have accompanied Jesus. We want to be a people who have walked with Jesus; we want to create a place where God may come to rest.

If we want God to reside with us, we must deal with our sin, our hidden sin. We'll have to let go of our carnal, fleshly desires. We'll have to give up our willpower and accept the spirit of judgment into our life.

We'll have to scream out in the same way that Isaiah did when he realized he was unclean in the face of the Lord.

6:5 (Isaiah) Then I exclaimed, "Woe is me!" Because I am undone; because I am a man of unclean lips, and I live among unclean lips; because my eyes have seen the King, the LORD of hosts.

The Lord will come to us, just as He did to Isaiah, to cleanse us and set us free from our hidden sins.

6:7 (Isaiah) And he put it in my mouth and said, "Look, this has touched thy lips; and thine iniquity is removed, and thy guilt is cleansed."

Our flesh must die while we are in the presence of God! We can't just brush things under the rug, forget about them, and then go to our hidden hideaway. Don't let sin fester in your heart; confront it. Prior to entering the glory, go to the mercy seat. When we make time and a secret spot to meet God, the dove of God will begin to rest. God's Shekinah Glory will come after we've provided a place for the Holy Spirit to remain. God's Shekinah radiance is the ever-present, apparent presence of Almighty. The Shekinah glory is a weighty glory that arrives in the form of a weight, a cloud, and a cloud. With the five senses of our natural existence, we touch, taste, see, smell, hear, and experience God's visible glory. The Shekinah always appears in the cloudy light.

Exodus 40:34, 35 The congregation's tent was then enveloped in a cloud, and the glory of the LORD filled the tabernacle. Moses was unable to enter the congregation's tent because the cloud had descended upon it, and the brightness of the LORD had filled the tabernacle.

The word for "dwell" and "glory" appears only once in the book of Exodus, and it refers to the manifest Shekinah dwelling splendor that you may touch, taste, see, feel, and experience in the natural world.

20:6 And Moses and Aaron proceeded from the congregation's presence to the congregation's tabernacle's door, and they fell on their faces, and the glory of the LORD appeared to them.

The glory was seen to everyone. It appeared like a cloud and a pillar of fire on the tabernacle.

When we prepare the sanctuary in a way that pleases God, I believe He will pour out His glory and live in our presence so passionately that we won't even have to speak. We'll walk into the building and be enveloped in the glory of God.

I believe there is a location where God's glory can shine so brightly that the ill are healed as we walk down the street.

25:22 (Exodus) And there I will meet with thee, and I will commune with thee from above the mercy seat, from between the two cherubims on the ark of the testimony, concerning all that I will command the children of Israel.

The cherubim are angels who guarded God's majesty. Those angles moved wherever God's splendour moved. They were a joy to be around, praising, adoring, and worshipping the Lord.

God, I believe, dwells in the praises of His people. If we wish to be in God's splendor and establish a home for Him, we must first understand what it means to praise and worship Him. This is about more than our worship time. I'm referring to the Lord's praise being in our mouth all of the time. Even when we don't say anything, our hearts are fixed in a worshipful attitude.

Praise will catapult us to glory. Praise will lead us to the Lord's throne room.

100:4 (Psalms) Be thankful to him, and bless his name, as you enter his gates with thanksgiving and praise.

But, do you know what occurs after you've been praised? This is something you must notice. We praise until Heaven's presence appears, and then we worship till the Glory appears! Praise will bring us to glory, but once there, we won't know what to do with ourselves. When we are lifted into the Glory by our worship, the first thing we do is receive God's goodness.

Now I'm basking in the glory! God is paying attention to me. We worship when we see the Glory for the first time.

I'd like to talk to you about the word "worship." "Adoration" is a synonym for "worship." I can worship for hours without saying anything. People sometimes ask me how I worship in this manner, and I tell them that it's like sitting at Jesus' feet, looking up at his face, and listening closely to Him. I'm standing in His splendor, admiring His beauty. I'm speechless in front of Him. I examine His features. This is worship, being motionless and silent. We stop chatting, we stop our activity, we stop entertaining, and we stop attempting to catch God's attention by speaking in tongues when we come into the glory of praise. When we begin to sense the presence of the Lord, we become still and worship.

Many Christians are coping with sin and constructing a place of worship for God. Is your worship fresh and new when God comes and looks at it? Is it the same old crap when God comes to your church?

You still want to be in charge of the meeting's flow, including how long the preacher will preach and how long you will worship. You still want to leave before noon since you don't want to offend any of your church's contributors. You still want to keep control of the manifestations and place them in the back room because you're frightened of offending some members of your congregation.

Some of us are constructing a sanctuary, but God is telling us that this is just another program, more of the same old things with a new twist. What happened to the stuff I designed? You built a refuge for Me, but you overlooked the revival pattern. You've designed church in a way that isn't in line with what I want it to be now. Even the way you preach and prophesy, as well as the manner you minister and manage church services, must change. We don't want to muddle things up! Some of God's plans are available to us, but not all. We won't be able to embrace the Holy Spirit if we continue to practice religion and control.

If we're watching things we shouldn't be watching in our hidden area, we won't be able to create an atmosphere that pleases the Lord. If we do, uncleanliness will permeate the sanctuary and pollute it. We also can't bring worldly vanities, consumerism, or apathy into the sanctuary. In the sanctuary, we can't combine the sacred with the profane.

Webster's Dictionary defines profane as "to regard sacred objects with disdain or contempt; to debase, pollute."

I know congregations who are experiencing revival and allowing the Holy Spirit to accomplish what He wants, but then squelch the Spirit's movement on Sunday morning. Every night during the week, there was a full-fledged revival! People were being saved, healed, and delivered, but there was no sign of the Holy Spirit acting on Sunday morning.

We've always completed the service at this time and dismissed the service in this manner.

If we don't modify the way we do things in Church and have a re-vival pattern, the sanctuary will be incomplete. And the things that come with the revival pattern will stretch us, cost us, insult us, and screw us up, but if we allow the Lord to refine and cleanse us, each hardship will work in our advantage. And when we delight God's heart by following His pattern with great care, we're displaying our commitment to Him. We're preparing for more than a visitation as we carry out God's instructions; we're preparing for a habitation for His presence.

Now I'll relate a revelation God gave me during the Litchfield Revival's early months. God mentioned an incense altar and the preparation of bread for Him. God revealed to me that if we do things in the natural to welcome Him, He will come and make our Church a home. You might be wondering why. If you do what you're about to read, I guarantee it will change your life forever. We had even set aside space in the Chapel and the dining room for God. We built an altar in the Chapel and burned incense on it.

We also made Him bread and sat in front of the Lord as a demonstration. We had a special table prepared for God in the dining room. We also baked bread and placed it in front of Him. God wants us to make spiritual and physical preparations in our life.

The Lord desires to live with us, and He desires for us to build a sanctuary for Him so that He may come and live with us.

He wants us to understand and follow His blueprints today, just as He provided Moses a blueprint for the tabernacle and its furnishings.

Exodus 25:8, 9 is a passage from the book of Exodus. And let them build a sanctuary for me so that I might live among them. You shall make it according to all that I show thee, following the pattern of the tabernacle, and the pattern of all its instruments.

The Holy Place was the first chamber, and it housed the table where the showbread was laid out, as well as the lampstand that shined on the showbread and the incense altar.

The Ark of the Covenant was kept in the second chamber, which was known as the Holy of Holies.

Incense Altars

Every item of furniture in the Holy Place was golden. The golden lampstand was on the left, the showbread table was on the right, and the golden incense altar was in the back, in front of the veil. The Holy of Holies was hidden behind the veil. Although the altar of incense is frequently associated with God's people's constant intercession, I believe it can also represent the crucified Christ who bled His blood for our sins. Also, I believe that the lack of an incense altar is one of the primary reasons why we do not have habitation in our churches today. The majority of today's churches do not even preach the truth of Christ's crucifixion and blood.

1:18, 19 in 1 Peter Because you know that you were not redeemed with corruptible things, like as money and gold, from your foolish speech passed down down the generations, but with the priceless blood of Christ, as of a lamb without blemish or spot:

Many Christians aren't even living the crucified life, much less laying down their lives for one another.

Philippians 2:3–4 Philipp Nothing should be done in a spirit of strife or vainglory, but rather in a spirit of humility, each should regard others as better than themselves. Look not only at what each person has, but also at what others have.

A gospel is being preached, but it isn't one of redemption and deliverance. God recently spoke to me and said, "Bill, I want you to think of all the churches you know." He asked, "Bill, how many church leaders do you know who can stand up and declare that people have been healed of tumors, deaf ears, and blind eyes in their services in the last year?" How many people can report that demons were thrown out of them right in the church when they were demonized? How many people have experienced salvation and deliverance?

I recall responding that I couldn't think of many churches that were experiencing miracles, however I could think of a few ministries.

The altar of incense represents both Christ's death and resurrection on the cross of Calvary, which has set us free from sin as well as deliverance and healing from our illnesses and maladies.

We are healed by His stripes. Today's church members are sick and diseased, and preachers are scared to speak about God's miraculous healing power or to lay hands on the sick! I know preachers who have maybe only touched five sick individuals in a year's time. Something isn't right. We don't have an incense altar, and we don't have crucified people! The altar includes preaching about the crucified Christ. Evangelism is also represented via the altar.

We won't be able to live unless we take the good news of the gospel that the Lord has entrusted to us and share it with a dying world.

If we don't share the good news of Jesus' salvation with the world, God will never dwell and let His splendor reside, settle, and remain with us. We won't be enjoying the good news if we never teach about the crucified Christ and aren't living examples of the gospel message. We will talk about healing and exhibit miracles, signs, and marvels as a sign that we are living and experiencing the good news.

Acts 10:38 How God anointed Jesus of Nazareth with the Holy Spirit and authority, and how he went about doing good and healing those who were plagued by the demon, since God was with him.

I know Christians who deny the existence of evil. They're suffering with disease and cancer, yet they're not praying for healing from the Lord!

There is no incense altar. Something has to be done. We need to start putting what we teach into practice! We must begin preaching the truth about Christ's cross and evangelizing.

Stop the bickering and politics, and get those who are going to hell inside the church. The lost must be welcomed and ministered to.

Showcase your bread

The bread of God's presence is the next topic I'd like to cover for your sanctuary.

Exodus 25:30 is a passage from the book of Exodus. And thou shalt always place shewbread on the table in front of me.

Leviticus 24:5, 6 is a passage from the book of Leviticus. And thou shalt take fine flour and prepare twelve cakes with it, each containing two tenth deals. And thou shalt arrange them in two rows, six to a row, before the LORD on the pure table.

That is why it is known as "showbread." Do you have any idea what the showbread symbolizes? Jesus is the star of the show.

6:51 John 6:51 I am the living bread that came down from heaven; whoever eats of this bread will live for ever; and the bread that I will give is my flesh, which I will give for the world's life.

For everyone, the showbread represents healing and deliverance.

Take a look at Matthew 15:22. And behold, a Canaanite woman appeared from the same coasts, crying out to him, "Have mercy on me, O Lord, thou Son of David; my daughter is grievously tormented by a devil."

Matthew 15:26 But he replied, "It is not proper to take the children's bread and throw it to the dogs."

She understood what He was saying and answered by adding that even the dogs eat the crumbs from the master's table.

So, what was her request?

She was praying for her daughter's healing and deliverance, exactly as He had done for the centurion's servant.

Matthew 8:13 (NIV) And Jesus said to the centurion, "Go your way," and "as you have believed, so shall it be done to you." His servant was also healed at the same time.

He was able to heal this woman's daughter.

Matthew 15:28 Then Jesus responded, saying to her, "O lady, great is thy faith: be it unto thee as thou desirest." And from that moment forward, her daughter was made complete. Healing and deliverance are the children's bread, and they are available to each of us in the Father's house.

Because Jesus declared, "Bread signifies provision," bread means provision.

Matthew 6:11 Give us our daily bread this day.

Because it is spiritual food, the showbread is also a revelation. We obtain revelation when we consume the bread of heaven, which is the Word of God.

As a result, the food of heaven is God's Word, revelation, the Lord's presence, healing and deliverance, and provision.

Do you have any idea what we did with God's bread? We've taken God's bread and replaced it with our own. This is how we went about it. We have programs instead of the bread of God's presence. We can go to our program and have Church instead of eating the bread of His presence. We also have gifted worship leaders, so if God's presence isn't present in the worship, the talent can fill in.

We have a worship concert and term it a divine action. We don't even expect God to appear since we assume He's already present, and we have no way of knowing that He isn't! He's not there because if He was, we'd have healing and deliverance bread as well. We would have a rich life if we were actually feasting on Him, and the bondage and poverty that exists in the church today would be gone. When we substitute the showbread with a gospel that says, "If you're sick, endure it; His grace is sufficient, and give Him glory in the midst of it, regardless!" we're eating white manufactured bread. The next day, that same individual is at the doctor, attempting to be healed of the ailment that God has bestowed upon them.

If that's our kind of faith, we shouldn't go to the doctor because we might be attempting to get rid of a disease that's supposed to be our thorn in the flesh (2 Cor. 12:7).

It is not true that sickness and disease are God's will and that we will be afflicted by them. Instead, we must believe that the Father actually knows what we require.

6:8 Matthew As a result, do not be like them; for your Father knows what you require before you ask him.

We've also done away with the surprise element. We've thrown away the showbread of revelation, exchanging it for information in the form of light lectures that don't convict anyone of sin but sound nice because they're full of emotionalism and hype. We've substituted intellect for God's word and revelation.

While I'm in the glory, I preach what the Holy Spirit gives me. I've prepared sermons that were flawless in form but lacking in glory. I'm telling you, I'd rather have the glory than flawless sermon points and sub-points.

We've exchanged God's Word for a collection of literature. I'm not suggesting that books are inherently bad, but some individuals refuse to even read their Bible. I would like for people to read my works, but I would also like to encourage you to read the Bible. People simply read one book after another. We accumulate so many books that the only revelation we have in our heads is what someone else has written. We haven't had any revelations because we haven't spent time in God's Word! We haven't had a lot of success.

"Bill, you must have read that guy's book!" people will sometimes say. "No," I respond. We are both filled with the same Holy Spirit.

That's a book I've never read." "Then where did you obtain that revelation?" they inquire. "I just got it from the throne, just like he (the author) did, and we both got it at the same moment because that's what God is speaking to us right now," says the author.

We've exchanged God's Word for knowledge. We must confess our sin of trading the showbread for this world before the Lord.

We'll need the showbread if we're serious about preparing a home for God. The incense altar is required, as is the ark, which includes the cherubim and the mercy seat.

Exodus 35:17-22 is a passage from the book of Exodus. The court's hangings, his pillars, and their sockets, as well as the hanging for the court's door, The tabernacle pins and the court pins, as well as their cords, The holy garments for Aaron, the priest, and the clothing of his sons to minister in the priest's office, as well as the cloths of service to do service in the holy place. And the entire congregation of the children of Israel left Moses' presence. And they came, every one whose heart was moved, every one whose soul was ready, and they brought the LORD'S offering for the work of the congregation's tabernacle, and for all his service, as well as the sacred garments. And they came, both men and women, as many as were willing, bringing bracelets, earrings, rings, and tablets, all gold ornaments, and every man who made a gold offering to the LORD.

Now let's look at what the apostle Paul wrote in Romans 3:23-25 about an important symbolic involving the mercy seat. For all have sinned and fall short of God's glory; being justified freely by his grace through the redemption that is in Christ Jesus: Whom God hath brought forth to be a propitiation through faith in his blood, to declare his righteousness for the forgiveness of past sins, through God's mercy;

Our mercy seat is Jesus.

According to scripture, the High Priest would enter the Holy of Holies once a year, on the Day of Atonement, and sprinkle blood on the mercy seat to atone for his and the nation's sins.

16:11-15 (Leviticus) And Aaron shall bring the sin offering bullock that is for himself, and shall make an atonement for himself and for his house, and shall slaughter the sin offering bullock that is for himself: And he shall bring it within the Vail, with a censer full of blazing coals of fire from the altar before the LORD, and his hands full of pleasant incense pounded small: And he shall light the incense before the LORD, so that the cloud of incense will cover the mercy seat on the testimony, and he will not die: And he shall take the bullock's blood and sprinkle it with his finger on the mercy seat eastward; and he shall sprinkle the blood seven times in front of the mercy seat. Then he shall slaughter the sin offering goat, which is for the people, and bring his blood within the vail, and sprinkle it onto the mercy seat and before the mercy seat, as he did with the bullock's blood:

16:30 (Leviticus) Because on that day, the priest will make an atonement for you, cleansing you from all your sins before the LORD.

The root of the words "mercy seat" and "atonement" is the same. It means to conceal, conceal, conceal, conceal, conceal, conceal, conceal, conceal, conceal, conceal, conceal, conceal, conceal, conceal, conceal, Jesus is our mercy seat, the Lamb, who spilt his blood on our behalf and atoned for our sins by dying on the cross in the greatest act of mercy ever performed.

We can come to Jesus Christ, the mercy seat, through faith to be forgiven of our sins and receive redemption.

Revelation 1:7 We have fellowship with one another if we walk in the light, as he walks in the light, and the blood of Jesus Christ, his Son, cleanses us from all sin.

Revelation 1:9 He is true and just to forgive us our sins and purify us from all unrighteousness if we confess our sins.

Revelation 2:2 And he is the atonement for our sins, not only ours, but the sins of the entire world.

Mercy wins out over justice!

2:13 James Because he who has shown no mercy will face judgment without mercy, while mercy rejoices over judgment.

We'll be ready to prepare a dwelling place for God when we experience a revelation of His ability to save and set us free.

A revelation regarding a lampstand and incense is also required.

Exodus 30:7–8 And Aaron shall burn fragrant incense on it every morning when he dresses the lamps; and he shall burn incense on it when he dresseth the lamps. And Aaron shall burn incense on the lamps at even, an everlasting incense before the LORD throughout your generations, when Aaron lights them.

He needed to refuel that lamp with fresh oil every day so it could continue to burn. Some of us, I see, don't have a lampstand. The lampstand provides illumination. The world's light is Jesus Christ.

8:12 (John) Then Jesus spoke to them once more, saying, "I am the light of the world; whoever follows me will not walk in darkness, but will have the light of life."

We don't have Jesus Christ if we don't have a lampstand! He is the Word of God.

1:14 (John) And the Word became flesh and lived among us, full of grace and truth (and we glimpsed his glory, the glory as of the only born of the Father).

As a result, we need to live a lifestyle that is nourished by God's Word, because the Word illuminates every element of our lives:

119:105 Psalms Thy word is a light to my path and a candle to my feet.

Every morning, we must tend to our lamp and burn incense. The incense is a symbol of prayer. The church must live a lifestyle that includes being immersed in God's Word, praying, and fasting. We will have habitation if we pray and have connection with God; if we have the showbread; the altar of incense; a sanctuary; the cherubim; and the mercy seat. We're preparing this place to receive the Lord's glory!

We must pursue the Lord's glory before it can ever remain. We can construct the sanctuary with all of the necessary furniture, but before the glory of God can descend upon it, we must have a burning desire to seek God, His presence, and glory.

3:1 And Joshua awakened early in the morning, and he and all the children of Israel left Shittim and traveled to Jordan, where they stayed before crossing.

Joshua got up early the next morning. The Israelites were preparing to cross the Jordan River. They would walk into God's promises and abundance once they had crossed the Jordan. They would arrive into the fruit, their inheritance, the land flowing with milk and honey. When they crossed the Jordan, Joshua gave the following instructions to the people:

3:3 Joshua And they gave the people orders, saying, "When ye see the ark of the covenant of the LORD your God, and the priests the Levites bearing it, then depart from your place and go after it."

The Ark of the Covenant was a visible evidence of God's presence that traveled with the nation of Israel, and the people were told to follow it.

I believe that our hearts must be totally engaged, on fire, and ready to pursue the Lord at all times.

If we want the Lord's splendor to dwell with us, we must take action and seek the Lord's presence. It's as if God is deafeningly deafeningly deafeningly deafeningly deafening But what He really wants is for us to be desperate for Him.

There was a moment when I was experiencing God's glory, signs, wonders, and revelation, and God told me that I wasn't hungry or desperate enough. I wondered at first, "What am I in your Glory?" I recognized after a while that there will always be a demand for more hunger and despair. We must continue to seek God.

The Ark of the Covenant must be transported according to the Lord's instructions, which King David and the Levites failed to recognize. Only the Levites, the priests, were chosen to carry the ark.

15:2 in 1 Chronicles Then David answered, None except the Levites should carry the ark of God: the LORD has chosen them to carry the ark of God and to minister to him forever.

The priests were expected to thread gold-plated poles through four gold rings at the bottom of the ark, then gently carry the Ark of the Covenant with the poles on their shoulders. Instead, they loaded the ark onto a fresh ox-drawn cart. David's experience can teach us a crucial lesson. When we long for the Lord's presence, we must respect His holiness and not allow our need to become familiar.

When God's presence approaches, we must also move out of the way and allow Him to come in His own time. David was enraged and terrified when the Lord judged Uzzah by striking him dead.

2 Samuel 6:9: Because the LORD had caused a breach upon Uzzah, David was displeased, and he named the area Perezuzzah to this day. That day, David was terrified of the LORD, and he said, "How shall the LORD's ark come to me?"

Look at 2 Samuels 6:10 As a result, David refused to bring the ark of the LORD into the city of David, but instead brought it away to the house of Obededom the Gittite.

If we pursue the ark, which represents the Lord's presence, He will reply. Manifestations will occur; God will move and speak in ways that may irritate us. We won't always be able to comprehend how individuals are affected by glory.

We won't always understand why God does things the way He does them or have all the answers. David was enraged because God did what he thought was out of character for Him.

"God acts in mysterious ways," I'm telling you, doesn't even come close to understanding His mystery. Many people will say, "I don't get why you're like that, God." So many churches want the spotlight to fall on them.

When revival comes with manifestations, however, and people respond in strange ways, trembling, falling, and reacting to the Spirit of the Lord, they think:

They wash their hands of it because they don't grasp this part of You, God. But David bounced back, even if he backed off for a bit (v. 11). We may fairly presume that their home was blessed because they possessed an attitude of reverence that stirred God's heart to bless them. The blessings were visible to David, and the fruit was good. As a result, he went after the ark once more, but this time with a renewed dread of the Lord.

Let's take a page from David's book. He did not give up, nor did he remain enraged and outraged. After all, he was the one who had angered God initially! So many of us have sought the Lord's presence only to be offended by something that has caused us to withdraw from the river of life. In our pursuit, something has slain us. It's possible that some of us sought God's presence and found it lacking in the ways we expected. Instead of God's presence, discouragement and tiredness have descended. Perhaps you've taken a step back, but now is the moment to return to the Lord. Have you insulted God in any way? We must recognize that God's ways are right, and that when we please Him, He will bless us since the fruit is good! His Presence is on its way!

Have you constructed a tent to house God's presence? Are you prepared to wait for the reward? Are you prepared to set up camp? We sometimes have to "go after it" by following God's lead. We must sometimes seek God's presence in our sanctuary. At other times, we must pitch a tent and wait for Him to arrive. Is it possible for you to construct a tabernacle within your heart right now?

Let's start looking into our hearts today. Examine whether you've prepared and built the furnishings in accordance with God's revival pattern. Perhaps you've given up some of the showbreads in exchange for that worldly religion: Bill, that's me. I've given up the food of His presence, the bread of His Word, and the bread of provision. Traditions, programs, and man-made means have replaced the bread of healing and deliverance in my life. Let us confess our sins now.

You must create a sacred place or a place in your life, a place in your house, a place in your church, and a place in your calendar if you do not already have one. He will come if you build it.

I want to settle down on you, God is saying! Don't be sidetracked from creating a dwelling place and seeking the Lord's presence.

I want you to consider your own life and ministry right now, and welcome the Holy Spirit's presence. I believe God is pouring out a deposit of His glory wherever you are reading this!

PRAYER

Father, I want to seek your presence and prepare a place for you to live. I beg your pardon for the times when you've arrived and I've been upset because I didn't understand or appreciate your ways. Lord, please forgive me.

I'm going to come to Jesus Christ's mercy seat. I desire You, God, and I desire to prepare a place for you to live.

Amen, in Jesus' name.

8

Keeping Going Despite Criticism

I've been in Revival for the past few years in the hopes of reaching God's heart for direction and insight for this year and the next decade. I was not let down! The significant revelation was made in relation to one of the most significant seasons in contemporary history. The Lord talked to me and told me that I was about to embark on the most crucial seven years of my life. It seemed as though everything I'd gone through in my life had been leading up to this moment. If that's true for me, I'm guessing it's true for a lot of you as well. Furthermore, the Lord made it clear that circumstances will determine how God's people seem in terms of maturity, strength, and authority. During this season, the spiritual darkness will reach such a height that only the Lord's people will be able to provide relief or resolution. We must fulfill our destiny as "priests and kings" to our God by becoming who we were created to be.

Revelations 5:9-14 is a passage from the book of Revelations. And they sang a new song, saying, Thou art worthy of taking the book and opening its seals: for thou wast slain, and hast redeemed us to God by thy blood out of every kindred, tongue, people, and nation; and hast made us kings and priests unto our God: and we shall rule on the earth. And I saw and heard the voice of many angels around the throne and the beasts and the elders, ten thousand times ten thousand, and thousands of thousands, saying with a loud voice, "Worthy is the Lamb who was slain to receive power, and riches, and wisdom, and strength, and honor, and glory, and blessing." And every creature in heaven, on earth, and under the earth, as well as those who are in the sea and all who are in them, heard me say, "Blessing, honor, glory, and power be unto Him who sitteth on the throne, and unto the Lamb forever and ever." Amen, said the four beasts. And the four and twenty elders prostrated themselves before him, worshipping him who lives forever and ever.

This text elucidates a number of spiritual dynamics that will play out in the next days:

It's a novel concept.

It's the exposing of what's been hidden.

It is for the benefit of the nations.

It entails the purchase of His blood as well as the harvest.

It makes it easier for His people to become rulers and priests.

Secrets & Mysteries

The Lord's unleashing of mysteries and secrets of His Kingdom that have been reserved for the end-of-time generation is the most important of these commands. The book of Daniel elucidates this paradigm. One of the most profound revelations ever offered to humanity was given to this great prophet. The angel that gave Daniel the insight, on the other hand, advised him to seal the book and keep the revelation hidden until the end of days. (12 Daniel)

This is a clear reference to the generation who will be alive on Earth at the time of the Lord's return. It would just take a small amount of effort to demonstrate that we are that generation. As the mysteries of those things formerly concealed are now exposed, we can expect tremendous revelation involving God's plans, purposes, and the uncovering of His Word in greater degree. The sealed book was opened by the Lord Jesus, and the contents were given to a group of people known as the Bride of Christ.

This company will appropriate their calling as priests and kings and facilitate the harvest once they have devoured this revelation. One of the fundamental obligations we carry as a ministry is to preach this biblical warning.

Between 2012 and 2015, there was an increase.

Surprisingly, the Lord also identified two prevailing adversary spirits who will be despatched this year and in the years ahead with the mission of obstructing this call. They are fanaticism and criticism, respectively. I observed these two spirits acting as bookends, coming from opposite directions yet with the same purpose to stop God's Kingdom's prophetic release and thwart the harvest. The first was a dark surge of fanaticism that will sweep behind the Kingdom truths to be disclosed, with the goal of pushing them beyond biblical boundaries and correct balance.

The Illusion of Fanaticism

"Wildly excessive or illogical devotion, dedication, our passion, an extreme zeal or enthusiasm as in religion or politics," is how fanaticism is defined.

Unfortunately, there are far more examples of spiritual frenzy in Church history than we could possibly mention. Every modern revival had a fanatical element to it. The prophetic movement has had its fair share of hype and extremism, which has effectively turned many people away from this critical part of our history. Nonetheless, we must heed 1 Thessalonians 5:19-21's admonition. Do not put a stop to the Spirit. Prophecies are not to be despised. Demonstrate everything; stick fast to what is good.

Because of the obsessive aspect that the more grounded Christians want to distance themselves from, this spirit seeks to drive things beyond biblical balance and sway people away from the basic truth. Of course, fanaticism must be defined in the context of a certain situation. Genuine Kingdom seekers will swing away from the truth to remove themselves from the fanatical element as a result of the frenzied spirit. That would be heartbreaking!

Historical Point of View

This remarkable comment about Martin Luther is recorded throughout history. Despite Luther's egregious errors concerning Israel and the Jews, it is a historical reality that God used him to initiate a great Reformation for God's people. Many historians amazed not at his ability to withstand his direct assault on the ecclesiastical organizational structure of the day, which wielded immense political power to expel its foes, but at his ability to keep his head above all the hysteria that surrounded his movement. My experience shows that many saints have a tendency to move away from extremely important truths that are about to be revealed today due to numerous fanatical aspects attempting to attach themselves to that knowledge. We must study the Scriptures, as the Bereans did, to see if these things are true.

We must embrace the balanced truth to become what we are called to be, notwithstanding the extreme aspect, if it is supported by God's Word and the Holy Spirit.

Criticism as a Spirit

Criticism was the second energy I saw coming from the opposite direction. "The act or occurrence of making an unfavorable or severe judgment, criticism, analysis, or interpretation of one's philosophy, doctrine, or life," according to the dictionary. According to what I've seen, this season will see even more vehement religious rejection to Kingdom truth in the hopes of repelling the advancing army. History is riddled with innumerable examples of uncompromising criticism of spiritual outpourings and movements, much like fanaticism. The Azusa Street Revival, the Latter Rain Revival, the Charismatic Renewal, and the Lakeland Outpouring were all examples of this.

As an individual, I would prefer to keep a safe distance from the fanatics than to succumb to criticism. Nonetheless, we must develop the same fortitude as the early apostles in order to usher in this new era and give to God's people revelatory truth that has been saved for our time. We are living in the time prophesied by Jeremiah in Jeremiah 33:3. Call upon me, and I will answer thee, and I will show thee great and wonderful things that you are unaware of.

As a result, it should come as no surprise that much of this truth stretches beyond traditional belief structures and into revelation. In this hour, the Word of God will be revealed on a scale never seen before in Church history. Daniel 12 and Revelations 10 both contain prophetic directives to this effect! It will hasten the powerful outpouring of God's people and make the harvest easier.

Despite spiritual opposition, including extremism and criticism, this prophetic promise will be fulfilled.

I want you to be encouraged and know that critics will come no matter how far you go in God's Glory. It makes no difference who is against you if God is on your side.

Seeing God's Glory for the First Time

As I share about God's desire to change our world via the presence of His splendor, my enthusiasm and hunger for God's glory will stimulate your zeal for reaching new levels.

Exodus 24:9, 10 are two verses from the book of Exodus. Then Moses, Aaron, Nadab, and Abihu, as well as seventy of Israel's elders, went up: And they beheld the God of Israel, and there was a paved work of sapphire stone beneath his feet, as well as the body of heaven in his clarity.

We are fortunate to have witnessed so many of Heaven's revealed signs and wonders. We are living in a day and hour unlike any other! Matthew 13:16–17 in Matthew Your eyes, however, are blessed because they see, and your ears are blessed because they hear. For verily, I say unto you, that many prophets and good men have wished to see what you see, but have not seen it; and to hear what you hear, but have not heard it.

Don't take anything for granted! Don't dismiss God's intervention in your life as a minor occurrence. God is about to do far more than we can imagine or ask. Anyone who has heard me preach in the last three years has heard me declare, "ON EARTH AS IN HEAVEN."

For the presence of God's glory is visible, and I want you to have a clear picture of what it would be like if the actual glory of God materialized in the room right now. God's visible magnificence, as seen in the supernatural encounter described in the preceding text from Exodus. Consider this: Moses, Aaron, Aaron's two sons, and seventy elders all witnessed the presence of God in Israel! Not only had "on earth as it is in heaven" become a reality, but so had "on earth as it is in heaven."

When Ezekiel beheld God's glory, he described sapphire stone over the cherubim's heads.

1:26 Ezekiel And there appeared a resemblance of a throne, as the appearance of a sapphire stone, above the firmament that was over their heads, and upon the likeness of the seat was the likeness as the appearance of a man above it.

10:1 (Ezekiel) Then I glanced up, and there, in the firmament above the cherubims' heads, there appeared over them as if it were a sapphire stone, with the appearance of a throne.

I'm starving for such a tangible manifestation of God's glory. It was seen by Moses and the seventy elders. Like when Isaiah saw the Lord sitting on His throne high and raised, and the train of His robe filled the temple, God's majesty descended into this earthly sphere, and there was no mistaking it.

"Holy, holy, holy is the Lord of hosts; the whole earth is full of His glory!" the seraphim exclaimed to one another.

6:1-3 (Isaiah) I also saw the Lord sitting on a throne, high and exalted, in the year that King Uzziah died, and his train filled the temple. The seraphim stood above it, each with six wings, two of which he used to hide his face, two of which he used to cover his feet, and two of which he used to fly. And one shouted out to another, saying, "Holy, holy, holy, holy is the LORD of hosts; the whole world is filled with his splendor."

There's so much more God has in store for us, and I want to go beyond just knowing God's serenity, as beautiful as that is, and into such grandeur, as it looked on Moses' face as he descended from Mount Sinai.

Do you think the realm will appear?

Isaiah 60:1-2 Shine, for thy light has arrived, and the LORD's splendor has descended upon thee. For behold, the earth will be covered in darkness, and the people will be in total darkness; but the LORD will arise upon thee, and his glory will be seen upon thee.

What would happen if the glory shone brightly in your eyes? Moses had to cover his face with a veil because the visible brightness was so brilliant.

34:33 (Exodus) Moses covered his face with a veil until he had finished conversing with them.

But here we are, in our modern-day religion, freaking out because a few people have a little gold on their faces! Stephen's face shined as well, and the Bible claims that it became as dazzling as an angel's.

6:15 (Acts) And everyone in the council, with their eyes fixed on him, saw his face as if it were the face of an angel.

It would be beneficial if our shadow had some solidity like

Peter's! When his shadow fell on some of the sick as he walked by, they would be healed.

5:15 (Acts) So much so that they dragged the sick out into the streets and strewn them about on beds and couches, hoping that the shadow of Peter passing by might at least cover some of them.

We also need something to happen when we stroll around, such as in the mall! Let's get this party started! I guess you can see I'm really hungry, desperate for more of that visible, wonderful realm of grandeur, sapphire, lightning, consuming fire, and angels to change everything around us! We're all seeing it at the same time! As it is in heaven, so it is on earth! Lord, please come!

The events that are about to unfold will be witnessed by many rather than a select few. During our meetings, in parking lots, on flights, and in restaurants, to name a few places, we will experience manifestations of God's splendor. Gemstones and gold dust from the Glory of God have appeared in restaurants, motels, and even the car. People are cured when the Glory of God appears! People are being rescued! People are growing in their sense of God's love for them.

84:11 in Psalms God is a sun and protection for the LORD: the LORD will grant grace and honor, and nothing good will he withhold from them who walk uprightly.

It's fantastic. Because Jesus is the same today as He was yesterday, and He will always be the same!

14:12 (John) True, true, I say to you, whomever believes in me will do the same works that I perform, and greater works than these, because I am going to my Father.

The splendor's nature The dazzling gold teeth, diamonds and gemstones from Heaven, feathers, or gold dust, to name a few, are frequently wrongly considered to be manifestations. These are indeed celestial manifestations that occur, but they are not the true splendor. They are an indication that God is present, and they stem from His love and nature. But, in the end, the Person, the inner Person of God Himself, is the true essence of God's grandeur.

I'm afraid that when God pours out His greater glory, the church will become so engrossed with the manifestations that come with it that they will forget about the Person. I was in the midst of a revival, and people were disappointed if there weren't mountains of diamonds. We sensed His awe-inspiring presence, and we need to know that the source is the Lord.

All of the other things happen when we go for God for Him. If you invite God in frequently enough, He will eventually move in.

God stated He was moving in our Church, where I had been a Pastor for nearly five years, at one point. It would likewise be a shambles, according to God. It would have a lived-in look, according to God. God came in, and man, did He come in. There was glory dust (of various colors) in practically every room and throughout the halls. It came in waves and eventually engulfed our Church. It was a shambles, just as God predicted. When you pursue God's glory, all of the other things will naturally materialize in a higher realm.

Because the term glory implies to exalt and bring honor, the glory of the Lord places you in a position of exalted honor, wealth, favor, and dignity. I was fortunate enough to receive this incredible favor. It appears that individuals would go out of their way to bless me. We required tens of thousands of dollars in donations from businesses and individuals. There were heaters in our rooms, as well as a music system and chairs.

Years ago, I received a Prophetic Word that God would exalt me if I humbled myself. It is a privilege to be a part of God's Glory. True recognition, receiving and supporting your ministry vision, and much more will all serve as evidence of this. People will recognize your position or rank, and you will get a spiritual crown of honor.

SHEKINAH AND KABOD

Let's take a look at two ways that God's grandeur is manifested.

When God's substantial splendour presence appears, it is called kabod—weight, grandeur (abundance).

Who can stay on their feet when this hefty kabod arrives?!

A heavenly "heavy-duty" experience is described in Scripture.

When the priests had exited the sacred place, the cloud filled the temple of the LORD. Since of the cloud, the priests were unable to minister, because the glory of the LORD had filled the house of the LORD.

Consider how substantial, plentiful, wonderful, and full of grandeur that glory is!

Shekinah:

Although this word does not occur in the Bible, it has a literal meaning of settle, live, or reside in Biblical Hebrew and is frequently used in the Hebrew Bible.

Exodus 40:35 is a passage from the book of Exodus. Moses was unable to enter the congregation's tent because a cloud had descended upon it, and the brightness of the LORD had filled the tabernacle.

Shekinah is the cloud here. The Shekinah is God's visible presence when He comes.

The Shekinah was described as a magnificent and glorious light engulfed in a cloud in every depiction. So, when the Bible calls it a pillar of cloud and a pillar of fire, it's separating what was once one into two? A pillar of fire and a pillar of cloud were always present. It refers to a light source. It's not simply a reflection of light, as when Moses reflected God's splendor and his face gleamed. The splendour of Shekinah is the wellspring of all illumination.

The light of His glory presence is the genuine entrance to supernatural encounters, and when the Shekinah glory arrives, you will have a route into paradise.

Job 38:19, 20 are two of the most important verses in the Bible. Where is the path that leads to the place where light dwells? And where is the land of darkness, that thou mayest carry it to the bound thereof, and that thou mayest know the paths leading to the dwelling thereof?

Job is being questioned by God about where light begins. He requests Job to bring the light to its region so that he might learn the roads leading to its home. Light has paths, and if you know what those paths are, you can follow it back to heaven. So there's something important about God's Shekinah splendour. It's the path to its home, where it was made and exists, and it's the very gateway, the very light, of who God is. God is light, and it is where we call home. In the glorious light, there are portals that lead straight to the sky.

19:1 (Psalms) Greetings, Chief Musician! A Davidic psalm. The heavens proclaim God's glory, and the firmament reveals his creation.

This splendour is a blinding white light that is magnificent, bright, and gleaming. It was the force of the Most High that "overshadowed" Mary, and she conceived Jesus Christ as a result of it.

1 Corinthians 1:35 The Holy Ghost will come upon thee, and the power of the Highest will overshadow thee; therefore, that holy thing which shall be born of thee shall be called the Son of God, said the angel.

When the Shekinah glory appears, it is a manifestation of power from on high that gives birth to things. When Peter walked by the sick, it was the centre of his shadow that healed them. The glory cloud, you see, has a healing miraculous anointing. Because the term glory implies "shade, covering, splendor, light, white, a cloud of His presence," it's the substance in which a glorious realm surrounding you provides miracles.

Do you aspire to live in glory closeness with God's inner self, rather than just knowing who He is and what He is? A deep longing to be the resting place for His evident presence, which manifests itself as heavy weightiness: kabod, and His visible presence, which manifests itself as Shekinah. You will be touched with the glory as a natural outflow of abiding in that miraculous location, and wealth, riches, exaltation, a crown of glory, and you will be glorified because of God's splendor presence. Intimacy with God is forgotten. When you pursue God in this way, your life becomes God's rather than your own. Nobody gets God's glory, signs, and miracles on a regular basis without paying a price.

Because he argued with God about it, Moses did gain a revelation about being marked by God's glory and presence. It meant everything to him! God opted not to accompany the children of Israel on the next leg of their journey into the Promised Land after they insulted the Lord by building a golden calf. He instructed Moses that instead of sending an angel before them, He would send an angel who would compassionately help them by driving out their adversaries.

Exodus 33:2 And I will send an angel ahead of thee to drive out the Canaanite, Amorite, and Hittite, as well as the Perizzite, Hivite, and Jebusite: I will not go up in the middle of thee; for thou art a stiffnecked people; lest I consume thee along the route.

God's supernatural powers, signs, and miracles are represented by the angel. God promised Moses the promised land, as well as all the signs and marvels that would accompany it. That's fantastic, and some people are content to leave it at that in their ministry. They camp out at the signs rather than teaching about the glory of who God is, His Person, and His presence. They teach about glory in terms of signs, but they've lost sight of what true glory is. It isn't a movement, and there aren't any signs. It is God's person, God's character, and God's own presence.

When we're in His presence, I value all the indications that appear! I want everything! However, this is not my main focus. Let's give Jesus our undivided attention! That's where I'm concentrating my efforts. I see signs and wonders all the time, and people react in such a variety of ways. The majority of what I perceive is based on erroneous motivations. I know that the majority of the Body of Christ has yet to experience the manifestations and is unsure how to respond. If gold dust and gemstones start falling, I'm sure a lot of people will hurry to pick them up. I feel that if we keep pressing in, the few indications will turn into numerous in minutes. The haste to obtain the signs suffocates the Holy Spirit even more. How much more could God accomplish if we continued to praise Him and focused on the one who brought the manifestations rather than the manifestations themselves?

Exodus 33:17, 18 are two verses from the book of Exodus. And the LORD answered to Moses, "I will also fulfill this thing that thou hast spoken," because thou hast found grace in my eyes, and I recognize thee by name. I entreat thee, show me thine glory, he said.

So, what is God's response to Moses?

Exodus 33:19 is a passage from the book of Exodus. And he said, "I will bring all my kindness before thee, and I will declare the name of the LORD before thee," and "I will be gracious to whom I will be gracious, and I will shew mercy on whom I will shew mercy."

We typically assume that the glory would come in the form of a miraculous manifestation, but God declares, "I will make all my goodness pass before you" (goodness, favor, and blessing). When the Lord's splendor appears, all of God's kindness will descend upon your life, affecting your business, wealth, reputation, and relationships. God's splendor is the literal weight of God's interior existence; personal awareness of God Himself; and God's inner person. His glory sweeps over you and settles on your life. I'm referring to the Father of Lights, who bestows every good and perfect gift, allowing all of His goodness, all of heaven's treasure, all of God's blessings, and all of His favor to pass before you.

God desires for the degree of brilliant glory inside you to outnumber the degree of darkness within you, allowing the light to possess you. Going higher and deeper in holiness, allowing God's presence to come and inspect our hearts, has a certain allure. When this occurs, you will be prepared to display God's evident splendor!

9

In the Glory of Sowing and Reaping

We'll look at various ideas in God's Word that teach about sowing and reaping in glory in this chapter.

This is a true idea that I have seen many ministers disregard. It has been omitted from the truth. I'd like to know that I'll provide you with scriptural foundations for Sowing and Reaping in the Glory. Those of you who are stuck in disbelief will be set free from that stealing spirit!

84:11, 12 Psalms God is a sun and protection for the LORD: the LORD will grant grace and honor, and nothing good will he withhold from them who walk uprightly. Blessed is the man who trusts in the LORD of hosts.

This is an exciting time to experience a new level of relationship and closeness with God! We've just stepped over a beautiful threshold! From this day forward, there is a real splendor with us, and it is bringing amazing favor and increase into our lives, the likes of which many of us have never seen or tasted before. I'm well aware that this is merely the beginning! What God is establishing in this hour is something far beyond than anything we could ask or imagine, so that we may always be assured that it is God's doing. It's in His time, and it's all because of His grace and glory.

God is keeping an eye on His word in order for it to be fulfilled. While we are pursuing God's Greater Glory, we are witnessing miracles being released. In our pursuit, we're also learning about the strategic value of sowing when in glory, since that's our anointed, the appointed time of holy visitation, the hour of visitation to obey the Lord and sow! God's favor is here because believers accept the Holy Spirit's promptings. Breakthroughs are unleashed, sometimes very rapidly, and believers reap the blessings that God has planned for them. Believers are given the opportunity to help others!

When Jesus Christ took hold of the Torah scroll in his hometown synagogue and read from the prophet Isaiah, he ushered in "the year of Jubilee."

Isaiah 61:1 Because the LORD has anointed me to preach good tidings to the meek, he has sent me to bind up the brokenhearted, to proclaim liberty to the captives, and the opening of the prison to those who are bound; to proclaim the acceptable year of the LORD, and the day of our God's vengeance; to comfort all who mourn;

4:14–19 Luke And Jesus returned to Galilee in the power of the Spirit, and a reputation for him spread throughout the region. He also taught at their synagogues, where he was praised by all. And he returned to Nazareth, where he had been raised, and on the sabbath day, he went into the synagogue and stood up to read, as was his tradition. And the book of the prophet Esaias was brought to him. The Spirit of the Lord is upon me because he has anointed me to preach the gospel to the poor; he has sent me to heal the brokenhearted, to preach deliverance to the prisoners, and recovery of sight to the blind, to set at free those who are bruised, to preach the acceptable year of the Lord.

25:10 (Leviticus) And you shall celebrate the fiftieth year, proclaiming liberation throughout the nation to all its inhabitants: it shall be a jubilee for you, and you shall return every man to his possession, and every man to his family.

The jubilee has arrived, and anointing is now available! It also applies to us. We can also say "Jubilee"! For example, there are moments when the Spirit of the Lord God is physically upon me, and He anoints me with an anointing with the intention of proclaiming "Jubilee!"

When that anointing is released, individuals enter what the Bible calls Jubilee, a year of liberation in which debts are forgiven, land is freed, and sons and daughters, captives and bounds, are supernaturally set free. That jubilee of liberation springs from the glory, from the presence of the glory. I'm referring to the anointing of glory, the anointing of glory!

This anointing of glory goes hand in hand with God's power that is beyond our comprehension.

I'm aware that the majority of Christians do not have a true revelation of God's goodness. I'm going to tell you about God's goodness. It will shatter some of your preconceived notions. Blessing is God's pleasure; it's who He is.

10:22 (Proverbs) The LORD's blessing makes one wealthy, and he adds no sadness to it.

The Lord's blessings are upon you! It's a rule of spirit.

60:3 (Isaiah) And the Gentiles will flock to thy light, and kingdoms will be drawn to the splendor of thy rising.

Paul's letter to the Ephesians (Ephesians 3:16) That he would strengthen you with might by his Spirit in the inner man, according to the riches of his glory;

God has anointed you with a mighty anointing, and it is according to the riches of His glory. Everything in God's provision is according to His glory riches! God want to provide all of your needs.

4:19 Philippians But my God will meet all of your needs through Christ Jesus, according to his riches in glory.

But don't put any restrictions on God! You may believe you just require a little, but God has much more in store for you! God rewards us because of who He is, not because of what we have, though he does sometimes multiply what we have. You'll discover that it's all about trusting the One who is present in your life.

3:20 (Ephesians) Now to him who, according to the power that works in us, can do exceedingly abundantly over all that we ask or think,

That's the anointing, that's the glory!

21:20 (Proverbs) In the wise man's house, there is a wealth and oil to be sought, but a foolish guy spends it all.

1:27 Colossians Whom God wishes to reveal the riches of this mystery's glory among the Gentiles, which is Christ in you, the hope of glory:

It's the anointing and the oil, and when you generously give the oil rather than squandering it, people are blessed, and you are blessed as well.

11:25 (Proverbs) The liberal (generous) soul will be fattened, and he who watereth will also be watered.

The anointing of glory will fall on you in a tangible way; your life will drip with dew, wine, and the oil of heaven. Because God wants us to have more than enough so that we might sow into the kingdom, take the nations, and expand the gospel, you will be blessed with the riches of glory.

Let us remember that this is accomplished by our obedience, love for God, doing our part, sowing as God directs, and reaping.

The apostle Paul explained this sowing and reaping link to the Corinthian church:

2 Corinthians 9:6-8 is a passage from the book of 2 Corinthians. But I say to you, he who sows sparingly will reap sparingly, and he who sows bountifully will reap bountifully. Every man should give according to his heart's desire; not reluctantly or out of necessity, because God loves a happy giver. And God may make all grace abound toward you, so that you may abound in every good work, always having all sufficiency in all things:

As a result, being a generous, happy donor allows God to reward you in a variety of ways so that you might bless others.

22:9 (Proverbs) Blessed is he who has a generous eye, for he gives of his bread to the needy.

If your heart isn't in the right place and you're giving simply because it's the Christian thing to do, it doesn't matter how much you give; the principle won't work for you! The mindset behind what you're pouring into the kingdom has to be one of joy, love, revival, generosity, and blessing.

In the Book of Acts, there is a wonderful picture of sowing with a righteous attitude. There was a revival after Pentecost, according to what we've read. People responded in a variety of ways, one of which was to spread glory! They sold their belongings and deposited the earnings at the feet of the apostle. But do you have any idea what caused that magical giving? It was an outpouring of the Holy Spirit. So that they may provide to the destitute on a daily basis. Their main focus was the spread of the gospel! And every day, God increased their number, and those who were being saved!

Lost souls are influenced when you have the power of God and the blessing of the Lord! The Lord's blessing comes when His splendour presence is at work. It will catch up to you! You have no idea what's going to happen! It's the Lord's blessing catching up to you in your debt. It's catching up to you in your enslavement; it's catching up to you in your lack! It's catching up to you in ministry! The stranded are being rescued! You're reaping the benefits! You can be ineffective even if you have no idea what you're doing! You aren't gifted in any way. But you can't fail when you have the Lord's blessing.

It's a force that will always lift you up, always propel you forward, always propel you into prosperity, always propel you into abundance. It comes not because you're brilliant, but because you have a heart that desires to please your heavenly Father, and you follow the Holy Spirit's direction!

You may be in a bad situation; you may feel powerless, but your deliverance will come if you have a heart that pleases God and seeks to Him for aid. Sometimes it's as simple as trusting and doing what you're told. You never know when God will use the prophets to settle a debt!

2 Chronicles 4:1–7 Now a certain lady of the prophets' sons cried out to Elisha, saying, Thy servant, my husband, is dead, and thou knowest that thy servant did fear the LORD: and the creditor has come to take my two boys to be bondmen. What shall I do for thee, Elisha answered to her? Tell me, what do you have in your house? And she responded, Except for a pot of oil, thy handmaid hath nothing in the home. Then he said, "Go, borrow thy neighbors' vessels abroad, even empty boats; borrow not a few." And when thou hast entered in, thou shalt shut the door behind thee and thy sons, and thou shalt pour into all those vessels, putting aside what is full. So she turned away from him and slammed the door behind her and her sons, who had brought her the vessels, and she poured forth. When the vessels were filled, she said to her son, "Bring me another vessel." And he told her that there was no longer a vessel. The oil, on the other hand, remained. Then she came to the man of God and told him. And he said, "Go, sell the oil, pay your loan, and live thou and the rest of your children."

He asked her what she had in her house, and she took what she had, which was simply a small jar of oil, and followed the prophet's directions. After everything was said and done, her oil had multiplied so much that she was able to sell gallons of it, pay off all of her bills, and still have enough money to live on!

There was a gentleman who attended the sessions. He arrived in desperate need of a miracle. He would come once a week and sow about 700 pounds of seed. He continued to come expecting to be blessed by the Lord. He had been diagnosed with cancer and was in desperate need of a miracle. After many months of coming in this manner, he stated that he had received everything he need, and that this man had been healed of cancer by sowing in the Glory. His faith and insight drove him to sow the way he did.

I think that people who sow in God's glory will have their debts forgiven. God's wonders are happening every day! Various people are being led by the Lord to sow financially in response to the Holy Spirit's prodding. God reacts in glory when we respond to the Lord and His word.

As I previously stated, there is a strategic time for sowing our financial and material resources: "when in the glory because that is our anointed, appointed time of holy visitation, the hour of visitation to obey the Lord and sow!"

I'm aware that many of you reading this Chapter are dealing with debt issues, some of which are pretty significant. Now I'd like you to comprehend my feelings. This is not something I boast about; no way! But, based on what I've seen, the Lord has anointed me to believe Him for debt forgiveness and supernatural supply, and I'd like to make it available to you today.

I'm not implying that you must invest in my ministry to receive the breakthrough I'm referring about. I'm saying you should sow where there is good fruit and trust that God's Word will not return void. Sow something from the heart that want to bless what is going on in the world. And if our ministry has been a blessing to you and your heart witnesses to our mandate to take the gospel to the countries for the salvation of souls, healing the sick, blessing the destitute, and helping the orphans, we would like to invite you to consider sowing into Revival Waves of Glory's ministry.

You are not attempting to purchase a miracle, nor are you attempting to purchase anything from heaven. But, just as the widow's small jar of oil was multiplied and used to cancel her debt and give an overflow, I believe the Lord desires to demonstrate His strength on your behalf and supernaturally provide for you as you obey what He says. Let us all trust in your miracle as you sow! Consider what the Lord would have you to do.

16:9 in 2 Chronicles Because the LORD's eyes go throughout the earth, he shows himself strong in the behalf of those who have a perfect heart toward him. Because you have acted poorly here, you will have battles from now on.

10

Enhanced Glory

The Church is about to go through something that no previous generation has ever gone through. You'll be elated to learn about the greater splendor being released right now, as well as how to prepare yourself to ascend further into this heavenly realm. The Earth is about to be covered in this amount of glory.

There is a priceless reward for those who meet God's divine conditions.

14:21 (John) He who has my commandments and keeps them is the one who loves me; and he who loves me is the one who will be loved by my Father, and I will love him and manifest myself to him.

The priceless reward is God's love and tangible presence! It's a spiritual union with the Holy Spirit. You may now be asking how God presents Himself to us or what His greater grandeur looks like. I'm going to tell you about something that happened in the larger splendor. I pray that you may be inspired to follow God and the great things He has planned for you this year!

There are certain ministers out there who are claiming greater glory for their presence. Others claim to experience third-heaven visits, but they don't. I want you to know that if somebody claims to be experiencing God, there will be fruit signs, wonders, or miracles. I'm wary of referring to something as greater glory if it hasn't yet reached that level.

Let's get started on this fantastic subject of more glory.

When you read through the Book of Ezekiel, you'll notice how the Lord's splendor left the city.

10:18, 19 Ezekiel Then the LORD's brightness descended from the house's threshold and stood over the cherubims. When they went out, the wheels were beside them, and everyone stood at the door of the LORD'S house's east gate; and the cherubims stretched their wings and mounted up from the earth in my sight.

In the spirit, Ezekiel was brought to several locations.

1 Ezekiel 11 Furthermore, the spirit took me up and carried me to the LORD'S house's east gate, which faces eastward: and I saw five and twenty men at the gate's door, among whom I saw Jaazaniah the son of Azur and Pelatiah the son of Benaiah, lords of the people.

37:1 (Ezekiel) The LORD's hand was upon me, and he carried me out in the spirit of the LORD, and he deposited me in a valley full with bones.

Ezekiel 40:1-2 The hand of the LORD was upon me in the fifth and twentieth year of our captivity, at the beginning of the year, on the tenth day of the month, in the fourteenth year after the city was smitten, on the same day, and brought me thither. God led me into the country of Israel through visions, and he placed me on a very high mountain, which served as the frame for a city to the south.

Ezekiel's hair entangled him, Ezekiel 8:3. And he took me by a lock of my hair, and the spirit raised me between the earth and the heaven, and led me to Jerusalem in God's visions, to the inner gate that faces north, where was the throne of the image of jealousy, which provokes envy.

Ezekiel 43:5 is a prophecy from the prophet Ezekiel So the spirit lifted me up and led me into the inner court, where the glory of the LORD shone brightly.

God wanted me to preach about being transported in the Spirit at one point. It was something I didn't want to do. I promised God that I would preach it if He gave me twelve scriptures to back it up. I could only come up with two examples off the top of my mind. I thought I was on God's good side. I was sitting with the Lord one day and he just started prompting me to look at scripture passages (some you just read above). I started reading what God had given me, and there were twenty-six verses regarding individuals being moved (there may be more). The point is that I preached the sermon because God proved it to be biblical to me. I want you to allow God to reveal Himself to you as well.

It's possible that what occurred to Ezekiel will happen to us.

I want you to know that I've had some incredible encounters. I once had a pillow war with the Lord, which resulted in the pillows bursting and me being coated in feathers. God talked to me and said that His wings were covering me.

Many times, when I bask in God's beauty, I'll sit back and recall those instances when God visited me, and it's as if I'm back there. I understand that God desires for us to pursue Him and the bigger things that He has planned for us, "the greater glory," and "the greater glory than these."

Let me pose a question to you: what does greater glory imply to you? Before you continue reading, consider this.

2:9 (Haggai) The magnificence of this latter home will surpass that of the previous, declares the LORD of hosts, and I will establish peace in this place.

It's about the saints, the body of Christ, receiving greater glory, and they will reflect God's brightness everywhere they go! That's a fraction of the bigger glory's appearance! It will be bigger than the splendour that God bestowed on the disciples on Pentecost.

Acts 2:14-18 And when the day of Pentecost arrived in full force, they were all in one spot. And then, out of nowhere, a sound like a strong rushing wind came from heaven, filling the entire home where they were sitting. Cloven tongues appeared to them, as if they were made of fire, and it sat upon each of them. As the Spirit gave them expression, they were all filled with the Holy Spirit and began to speak in different languages.

We must have a pure heart! Unfortunately, the majority of the church is not ready for greater glory.

Those who are ready, who have had the Spirit of holiness work in their hearts, have been stripped. They are able to take in more and reflect more of God's glory. When your face is in front of the face of the Son of Righteousness, something happens. There will be a reflection, but don't be surprised. There isn't anyone walking around with the same radiance of brilliance that Moses possessed when he descended from Mount Sinai.

34:29 (Exodus) And it came to pass that when Moses descended from Mount Sinai with the two tables of testimony in his hand, Moses was unaware that the skin of his face shined while he conversed with him.

As a result of the deep work that God had done in Moses' heart, he could withstand a higher degree of the holy manifest dread of the Lord and the presence of the Lord. How many of you wish you had a greater ability to receive God's revelation without it destroying you?

1 Corinthians 1:1-6 Paul, a servant of Jesus Christ, an apostle, separated unto the gospel of God, (which he had promised afore by his prophets in the holy scriptures,) Concerning his Son Jesus Christ our Lord, who was made of the seed of David according to the flesh; and declared to be the Son of God with power, according to the

spirit of holiness, by the resurrection from the dead: For obedience to the faith throughout all nations, for his name, by whom we have received grace and apostleship: among whom are ye also the called of Jesus Christ:

In this critical hour, the body of Christ is preparing to receive God's magnificent grace in order to achieve the great things He has called us to do, all with a pure heart! While some of you are just getting started with this, others are far into it, and still others are in the right place now to be released into the bigger works.

These "greater works" will shine even brighter, or be even more impressive, than any of Jesus' miraculous deeds!

14:12 (John) True, true, I say to you, whomever believes in me will do the same works that I perform, and greater works than these, because I am going to my Father.

The saints will carry out the great tasks that God has called Christians to do, as well as the larger acts, by displaying God's glory wherever they go. That is an element of how the bigger brilliance will appear. It will be bigger than the grandeur that God bestowed upon the Early Church.

It's important to remember that holiness and purity of heart are prerequisites for this commissioning. I believe that if the same glory that God poured out on the day of Pentecost rained on us today, believers like Ananias and Sapphira would perish.

As a result, we must allow the Holy Spirit to work deeply in our hearts. I'd like us to look at Romans 1:1–6 once more.

1 Corinthians 1:1–6 Paul, a servant of Jesus Christ, an apostle, separated unto the gospel of God, (which he had promised afore by his prophets in the holy scriptures,) Concerning his Son Jesus Christ our Lord, who was made of the seed of David according to the flesh; and declared to be the Son of God with power, according to the spirit of holiness, by the resurrection from the dead: For obedience to the faith throughout all nations, for his name, by whom we have

received grace and apostleship: among whom are ye also the called of Jesus Christ:

The Spirit of holiness is the Holy Spirit working in you to make you holy, and you are being made holy as you obey what His voice in you is saying. You won't be acting in your flesh or by your carnal nature if you're operating in obedience to the Spirit of holiness as it flows through you.

The same Spirit that the Father used to bring Jesus from the grave was used to raise Jesus from the dead.

Romans 1:3, 4 Concerning his Son, Jesus Christ, our Lord, who was born of the fleshly stock of David; And by the resurrection from the dead, he was declared to be the Son of God with authority, according to the spirit of holiness:

The power of God and the resurrection of the dead both act through the Spirit of holiness in some way.

The power to bring actual resurrection from the dead, I believe, is the more excellent glory, and it reveals itself in the authority level that demonstrates the power. How many of you want to see super-human power like that?

This (higher glory resurrection power) isn't limited to literally reviving individuals from the dead. That's part of it, but it also includes kingdom domination, kingdom authority, a realm of the glory that comes in with a shattering atmosphere, and a tangible corporate presence that, for example, takes over entire city blocks. It's a sphere where revelation comes not just through the spirit of prophecy, but also through splendour.

1:17 (Ephesians) That the Father of Glory, the God of our Lord Jesus Christ, may give you the spirit of insight and revelation in the knowledge of him:

It's about God's displayed glory being so great that revelation occurs only as a result of the glory, not as a result of a gift, a spirit of prophecy, or a gift of prophecy. It just appears out of nowhere.

Out of splendour, miracles and healing occur! The Lord's healing power is just waiting to be used! I envision it as a great dimension of palpable corporate anointing descending in tiers and becoming a heavy resting glory in areas, cities, city blocks, and even entire cities! What is in heaven begins to appear quickly and effortlessly in our world. It just appears!

6:10 in Matthew Come, thy kingdom. As it is in heaven, thy will be done on earth.

When God pours out his splendor without real holiness and real fear of the Lord, true resurrection will not take place in this coming revival.

God desires to develop a generation of eagle warriors. This is a group of godly men and women who have God's glory streaming through them. Those who are anointed for supernatural signs and wonders and will travel across the planet with actual kingdom power!"

God's greater splendor isn't going to be everywhere; it's only going to be in a few regions, a remnant of places, where God is pouring out His glory. This greater splendor will come, but I am speaking in terms of the coming years. There is a manifest dimension of more splendour than we've ever known, and it will reveal itself in surprising ways. God is anointing the warrior's eyes right now in the spirit." I want to underline that God is providing us with the anointing for "eyes to see" right now! Many of us, understandably, are longing for this realm. We'd like to learn how to see in the spirit world. We want the domain of the unseen to open up. We desire the seer gift, as well as the ability to be visionary and have prophetic dreams and visions. Allow my eyes to be anointed and for me to see! Isn't that what you're crying about?

22:22 in the Bible And God's wrath was aroused because he went; and the LORD's angel stood in his way as an opponent against him. He was now riding on his ass, accompanied by his two attendants.

According to Scripture, the angel that stood in the way of Balaam and his donkey was an enemy of his. Because of his wickedness, Balaam lost favor with God.

22:34 in the Bible And Balaam replied to the angel of the LORD, "I have sinned; for I had no idea that thou stoodest in my path against me; now, if it displease thee, I will fetch me back."

He lost his spiritual edge and spiritual sight, and he didn't see the angel with his sword drawn until the Lord opened his eyes.

22:31 in the Bible The LORD then opened Balaam's eyes, and he saw the LORD's angel standing in the path, his sword drawn, and he bent down his head and fell flat on his face.

We won't be able to see what's going on in the invisible realm unless we have the eyes of eagle fighters or the anointing of God to see! We don't want to be in the same wicked state as Balaam, because God enjoys anointing us with spiritual sight when we have a clean heart. Today, I think God is anointing the soldiers with His anointing! What you are about to enter and what the church is about to enter is already happening, and you must be cautious because it is only now being released. It's a dimension in which the realm of glory will descend and heaven will become so real on Earth that angels will appear as men and you will be able to sit on a chair and have a conversation with them.

13:2 in Hebrews Don't forget to entertain strangers, as some have unwittingly entertained angels.

My engine blew one day as I was driving into my driveway. A man appeared out of nowhere, offering to assist me in pushing it into the driveway. We were able to park the automobile in my driveway. This man had a gruff appearance. He stated that he had an engine for my automobile and that he would assist me in replacing it. He indicated that the engine had roughly 50,000 miles on it and that he would like $50 for it. I agreed that he would show up the next day and start working. He did almost all of the work himself.

It was completed in two days, working only a few hours each day. I observed this man easily lift a four-cylinder engine and place it in the bolt holes. He finished and told me he was finished. He didn't even make an attempt to start it. I offered him $50, but he replied no, he didn't want it. I insisted, but he refused, stating that if you force it on me, you will not like me. I said okay, and he was gone before I realized it. When I went to the address he gave me, it was a vacant trailer. I feel this man was a divine messenger.

So that you know, I started the car, and it began right up. It is still operational today, despite the fact that it was created more than five years ago.

Angels are on their way, just like the men who accompanied the Lord to Abraham. They could have destroyed Sodom and Gomorrah!"

During all of this wonderful Glory and manifestations, the Lord's sword is coming to judge the supernatural in the church today, and something in the name of the supernatural will be cut off. The angel's sword is drawn, according to him, to judge the purity and motivation of how and why we function in the supernatural.

God is going to restore a pristine magical river! The greater glory has to come from the Holy Spirit!

22:38 in the Bible And Balaam replied to Balak, "Behold, I come unto thee: have I now any ability to speak?" I will say the word that God has placed in my mouth.

Similarly, we must behave in absolute obedience to what the Holy Spirit, the Spirit of Holiness, tells us to do or say. I'm only allowed to say what God tells me to say. It all boils down to honesty and obedience.

I think that by deciding to set our faces into God's holy wind, the Holy Spirit will blast out those things in our souls that are offensive to Him. Let us then ask the true Spirit of the Lord's fear and the true Spirit of purity to come into our hearts. Then we'll be able to follow the glory cloud of God and His greater splendour!

The most incredible prophesies sometimes occur in the most improbable of circumstances.

Following Israel's Babylonian captivity, the remnant who witnessed Solomon's Temple's magnificence and splendor may have found it difficult to trust Haggai's prophecy: Haggai 2:2-9 Tell Zerubbabel the son of Shealtiel, the governor of Judah, Joshua the son of Josedech, the high priest, and the rest of the people, "Who among you has seen this house in its initial glory?" And how do you think it's going now? Isn't that, in your opinion, nothing in comparison? But now, saith the LORD, be strong, O Zerubbabel; and be strong, O Joshua, son of Josedech, the high priest; and be strong, all ye people of the land, saith the LORD, and work: for I am with you, saith the LORD. My spirit remains among you, according to the word that I covenanted with you when you came out of Egypt: fear not. For thus says the LORD of hosts: Yet once, for a brief moment, I will shake the heavens, the earth, the sea, and the dry land; and I will shake all nations, and all nations' desire shall come: and I will fill this house with splendor, said the LORD of hosts. The silver and gold are mine, declares the LORD of hosts. The magnificence of this latter home will surpass that of the previous, declares the LORD of hosts, and I will establish peace in this place.

Nothing has ever equaled to the magnificence of Solomon's Temple, either before or since. This amazing prophecy foreshadows a time of immense restoration and promise. Many people today still find it difficult to imagine that the splendour of this modern church will surpass that of the early church. God, on the other hand, has promised it, and His Spirit will see it through.

In these final days, God will abide in a group of humans to display His holy character and do feats unprecedented in human history. We must start preparing for this eventuality.

A small group of people were inspired by Haggai and Zechariah's predictions to fulfill God's Word. One of the great promises is contained in the book of Zechariah, which states:

4:10 (Zechariah) Who has forgotten the day of simple things? They will exult when these see the plummet in Zerubbabel's hand with those seven; they are the LORD's eyes, which run to and fro over the entire earth.

Grace Grace has arrived.

We are surrounded by great grace.

We are surrounded by great power.

This indicates that the anointing, power, and authority exhibited by the Lord Jesus Himself to lay the foundation for the Church will be demonstrated once more at the end of the age to bring the capstone or ending of church history and the advent of the Kingdom realm.

What is the best way to accomplish this? Only via incredible and outstanding favor, accompanied by screams of grace.

The Tabernacle Feast is a spiritual precursor of this reality, depicting God's evident presence operating through a sold-out radical group of people known as the Bride of Christ. As the leaven of tradition and man-made doctrine is removed, this season will see huge demonstrations of the Spirit of Truth. The Spirit of Truth is collaborating with an angelic host to establish revelatory truth in the hearts of believers and the nations of the planet. Our goal must be to keep following the Word as it continues to flow from the Father's heart.

4:12 in Hebrews For the word of God is swift, powerful, and sharper than any two-edged sword, penetrating even to the dividing asunder of soul and spirit, joints and marrow, and a discerner of the heart's intentions and purposes.

This is a physical manifestation of God's presence. It's not a place where we give lip respect to things that aren't in line with our hearts' wishes. In the previous generation, we witnessed a tremendous illustration of this truth when anointed vessels stood before God's people and revealed heart secrets known only to them and God. This was more than just a lovely spiritual gift; it was a sign of the end-of-the-world scenario, when God takes up home in a group of individuals to accomplish larger things. Our advice is to collaborate (cooperate) with Heaven and only do and speak what we see the Father doing and hearing. The Lord is expanding our eyes and ears with the spirit of insight, allowing us to increase our discernment in order to attain this goal. Today, virtuous leaders who will be shepherds of love and truth will emerge. They have no intention of harming or abusing the sheep. Many of these leaders will have experienced both failure and tremendous restoration, as well as heavenly love. They will have been cleansed of their sins, but repentance will have become their standard in the process. The virtuous shepherds will bring the sheep to safe waters, allowing the body of Christ to experience God in new ways. Many of the shepherds will emerge from remote and inaccessible locations. They will carry authority to speak into people's hearts and will bring an anointing to calm the Church's tumultuous waters. The process of preparation has been lengthy and challenging, but God has given us new life at various moments to encourage us to keep pressing into Him. The Lord of the Harvest has now appeared. The harvest of souls and the harvest of promises begin with the humble and contrite, with those who tremble at His Word.

Isaiah 66:1 "The heaven is my throne, and the earth is my footstool," declares the LORD. "Where is the house that men build for me?" And where will I be able to rest? For all those things have been fashioned by my hand, saith the LORD; but to this man will I look, especially to him who is poor and contrite in spirit, and trembleth at my word.

For This Generation, Standing in the Gap

The Lord's eyes are roving the land, looking for a righteous person to stand in the breach. Is there no one there when I call, as the Lord asks? A small number of people on the planet will hear and respond to this appeal.

50:2 (Isaiah) Why, therefore, was there no one there when I arrived? Was there no one there when I called? Is my hand so shortened that it can no longer redeem? or do I lack the ability to deliver? As a result of my reprimand, the sea has dried up, and the rivers have become a wasteland; their fish stinks because there is no water, and they die of thirst.

Things can change swiftly when God's Spirit is present. He is giving His people a taught tongue so that a word from Him can sustain the weary. He is currently reawakening many saints morning by morning in order to give them eyes to see and ears to hear instruction, just as He did His disciples. Despite their folly, Job's holy prayer intervened for others around him. It's past time for God's people's fortunes to be restored as well.

When Job prayed for his companions, the Lord turned his captivity around and restored him twice. The season of the double portion is upon us.

Job 42:8 says: Therefore, take seven bullocks and seven rams, and go to my servant Job, and offer a burnt offering for yourselves; and my servant Job shall pray for you; and for him will I accept: lest I deal with you according to your folly, in that ye have not spoken of me the thing that is right, as my servant Job has. So Eliphaz the Temanite, Bildad the Shuhite, and Zophar the Naamathite went and did what the LORD had commanded them, and Job was accepted by the LORD. When Job prayed for his friends, the LORD turned his captivity around, and the LORD gave Job twice as much as he had before.

Many Christians are nearing the end of a period of pruning and judgment. As many people head our way in this gloomy season,

God's desire is for our light to shine brightly. It is now time for those who have triumphed to be crowned with a portion of His glory.

12:3 Daniel And those who are smart will shine brighter than the sun, and those who lead many to righteousness will glow brighter than the stars for all eternity.

It's time for divine plans to be fulfilled and a harvest to be reaped. This generation of young individuals, as well as the seasoned and mature, has been claimed by the Lord. Both Joshua and Caleb will be involved. In a third-day harvest of the wounded and persecuted, the Lord is repairing the rift He has created. His will is being carried out in a powerful fashion so that a crop might be reaped. Trials on the planet will get more severe, as end-time realities from the book of Revelations become more apparent. The Church will be given a great deal of insight into these secrets.

Revelations is a love letter to the Lord's bride, preparing her to be united with Him. We are doomed to succeed. The opponent has already been defeated by the Lord, who has created a public spectacle of him.

When we are linked to the Lord, He delegates His victory to us. One of our most important responsibilities in this hour is to cease being the Lord's servants and instead become His friends. To completely activate our faith, we need a clearer picture of our Friend who is eternally seated on His throne of victory and dominion. As God's word promises, commissioning from the Throne Room can be a live reality. He's yelling, "Come up here!"

The Lord's Church must be able to identify the periods and seasons, as well as possess Christ's mentality for this day. Anything is not His intention to keep it hidden from us, but rather to show profound understanding so that the world may witness God's blessing and wisdom on His people. The agony of our past serves as a springboard for our future. Hopelessness generates brokenness without the spirit of understanding, while brokenness with understanding imparts the hope of our calling in God. In order to introduce His own pure nature, the Lord's Spirit has been pruning and uprooting our fallen nature and carnal plans.

His ultimate goal is to show God's Fatherhood and to mature us as His sons and daughters. Despite the fact that we appear to have failed in many ways, these years have instilled humility in many. The fleshly arm and our own might are incapable of fulfilling the end-of-the-world mission. It will be through His Spirit alone, not through man's might or our own inventiveness.

It is our responsibility to yield and learn to work with Him. The Lord, like Jacob, has transformed our nature by destroying our reliance on human might.

2:17 (Revelation) He who has an ear, let him hear what the Spirit says to the churches: To him who overcometh, I will give secret manna to eat, and a white stone with a new name engraved on it, which no one knows save the one who receives it.

Isaiah 59:20–23 And the Redeemer will come to Zion and to those who repent of their sins in Jacob, says the LORD. My spirit that is upon thee, and my words that I have set in thy mouth, shall not depart from thy mouth, nor from the mouth of thy seed, nor from the mouth of thy seed's seed, says the LORD, from henceforth and for ever.

11

The Glory River

What do you want to get out of your Christian life? Are you seeking signs, wonders, and miracles, as well as healing, deliverance, liberation from poverty or lack, and a soul harvest for your city? If you aren't experiencing these manifestations of God's power in your Christian walk, ask God what He desires. It may surprise you to learn that there is one thing God wants you to cry out for beyond all else, and that is His glory.

God desires for you to be thirsty for His glory. There is one thing that God demands of His people above all else. That is what it is to be aware of His presence. He wants us to be aware of His presence in our life, and He is truly urging us to recognize that He is with us.

God's presence is a manifestation of His glory, and He is inviting us to drink from the river of His glory. More than anything else, I appreciate God's river of Glory. On this subject, I've released two full CD albums. Everything we require can be found in the Glory. The Soaking CDs dictate a lot of the writing in this Chapter. At the end of this book, you'll find a list of my suggested products.

God want for us to be hungry, frantic, and envious of His presence. He performs everything in the light of His glory. It's there that the power is. The brilliance, the glorious river of His presence, is where the power is.

Are you aware of God's glory in the way that God desires you to be aware of it? God desires to shower you with His blessings! Everything you do will be flooded, saturated, and covered. He's summoning His people to the river, to the glory. Everything He does is influenced by the water. That river will be the source of everything God will do.

Do you require medical assistance? Take a dip in the river of His majesty. That's where the creative miracles happen, where the blind see, the deaf hear, and the dumb speak, where broken hearts repair, and disease fades. Are you in a battle for the harvest? Get in the river and soak in the majesty of God. There is an abundance of harvest, not just one or two. Are you enslaved? Take a plunge into the river. Make a big impression. Are you in desperate need of a cash miracle? Go for a swim in the river. There's evangelism, joy, and sins being washed away in the magnificent river of His presence. We are set free from sickness, disease, sin, lack, and bondage when we face the glory of the living God, the glory presence of Jesus the Healer.

All that God asks of us is that we go deep, deep into His splendour, deep into the river of His presence. The river is the source of power. Everything is in the river. You are being drawn to the river by God. He wants you to want that spot more than any other place or thing. And you will see Jesus' face when you long for, hunger for, and thirst for His presence.

In a fresh, new way, God's splendor is emerging on the planet and in the lives of hungry Christians. Desperate believers, I believe, will enter the Lord's glory and see Jesus as they've never seen Him before. They will have a face-to-face conversation with God. You will understand the power of His resurrection when you know Him and are consumed with this one thing, that you would know Him.

3:10 Philippians That I could know him, and the power of his resurrection, and the camaraderie of his sufferings, as I am conformed to his death;

It will simply take place. Because God will trust you with it, you will simply manifest God's power wherever you go. You are being drawn to the river by God.

The river flows from God's throne in heaven, where He is present. If you want to see the river, you must first compete for the source's presence by situating yourself in front of the Throne. Place yourself in front of the One who is Life and the Anointing. Get into God's glory, into a relationship with Him, and into knowing Him. More than hungering for His power or the work of His hand, this is hungering to be in His presence. Above all, it is a hunger for Him. We prioritize other things, but the Bible commands us to do so (Matthew 6:33). But seek first the kingdom of God and his righteousness, and everything else will be added to you.

God is requesting that we seek Him out.

Many people have a relationship with God, yet they are unaware of His glory or intimacy. The glory of God can be seen in my bedroom at times. Knowing the glory means knowing Him for who He is, the deep reality of who He is, rather than knowing about Him. I'm talking about knowing the Lord's glory in such a way that His presence is as thick, rich, and heavy as honey. It's the kabod, the Lord's mighty brightness. We come to a point when we want His glory more than anything else, and we want to be with Jesus, since the Lord's splendor is His actual presence in Jesus. The Hebrew word for glory is kabod, which literally means "weightiness" or "substance." God has a heft, a density, and a substance that can't be found anywhere else. His majesty is massive and awe-inspiring. When David Herzog arrived to minister at the church where I was the pastor, this glory struck me. It was right before the meeting, and I was hit so strongly by the Glory that I fell off my feet and landed on my back, dripping gold dust.

I may have stated this in a prior Chapter, but it bears repeating. God spoke to me in the midst of revelations, signs, wonders, and miracles. "You're simply not hungry or desperate enough." I want you to desire Me above all else." You'll always need more of God, no matter how hungry you are for Him.

Remember that I was a minister for many years and had no feelings. Believe me when I say that once you experience God's glory, you will never be the same.

We must desire this imposing presence, this river, above all else. We must rely on Jesus to live. It isn't the same as having vision. I enjoy vision and sometimes think that as long as I have it, I can keep going, but it's a dangerous zone to be in. Living on Jesus is the only way we can keep going, the only way we can fully live. Vision, displays of power, daily, dutiful devotions, words of prophesy, and nothing else can sustain us but desperation and hunger for the glory. Our lives are guided by our appetites. When you can guzzle down God's grandeur, why sip? Is your hunger for God being replaced with a deep desire for anything of this world? Hunger for anything other than Him is perilous. The only thing that guarantees triumph is a thirst for God. Take a deep breath of God's magnificence. Taste the Lord and see how delicious He is.

God's grandeur is being revealed in the church. The glory cloud has appeared. It's happening with gold dust, oil, dental wonders, gold flakes, and feathers. The splendour of Shekinah is approaching. I promise you that the world will experience the sweeping power of Jesus' majesty, and the Shekinah will change people in an instant.

Are you familiar with the Shekinah? Shekinah is a Hebrew term that denotes God's visible presence. His people are aware of His presence.

8:11 in 1 Kings Since of the cloud, the priests were unable to minister, because the glory of the LORD had filled the house of the LORD.

The Shekinah Glory is a term used to describe this presence. Do you have any idea what happens when you enter the Shekinah? You transform in an instant. The Shekinah splendour is a spectacular display of God's brilliance, light, and fire. One encounter with the Shekinah, the manifest weight of His splendor, transforms you quickly.

The brilliance is the heavenly environment. The splendour is the atmosphere in which God lives.

As believers, the supernatural will become natural real, a daily occurrence in all we do and wherever we go. God and His kingdom can reveal themselves in such a way, and Jesus can change the spiritual environment of a gathering, a city, a region, or a nation! I believe there is a place where you can go deep enough into the realms of glory and stay there for as long as you want the Shekinah glory to fill and refill you. When you pray, seek only the glory, and you'll be so full with it that you'll carry it about for everyone to see.

All I wanted to do after seeing His magnificence was brag about it! When I tried to preach on something else, glory poured forth from my tongue! For months, I preached and talked about holy hunger, desperation, and desiring God's presence, and I'm still preaching it! I preached approximately fifty sermons on God's Glory in six months.

What is your level of desperation? Are you willing to go to any length to be in God's glory, even if it means waiting months for the glory to touch you? Some people expect preachers to simply give us a dose of glory, but that isn't how it works. You must hunger, thirst, and want glory, and this usually takes place in a solitary spot away from distractions. You won't have to care about what people think of you, and you'll be able to let go and go all out for God in your desperation. You can seek His glory in any location. Seek His majesty. Nothing else matters if you have His face, His kiss, and the river of His glory present.

God is growing up a generation of people who are more concerned with His face than with His hand or power. He looks for people who put Him first in their lives, who want to know Him and crave His presence more than anything else. You will see the face of Jesus when you desire for Him and pursue godliness! It's time to climb to the top of the holy hill and meet Him. Stand where the river of His splendor runs in the holy place. Everything you've ever needed can be found in the Glory. One look at the King of Glory will change your life for the better.

24:1-3 (Psalms) A Davidic psalm. The land, with all its fulness, is the LORD's; the globe, with all its inhabitants. Because he built it on the waves and established it on the floods. Who will ascend to the LORD's throne? or who will be the one to stand in his holy place?

The Lord want to take us to greater heights of splendor. He is inviting us to enter the river of His presence. It is His wish for us to be enthralled by the beauty of His face and to dwell in His majesty. The river of God's splendor pours from the Throne on High, where He dwells and where He is present. Under His shrine, a river springs up.

Ezekiel 47:1–12 is a book written by the prophet Ezekiel. After that, he led me back to the house's door; and behold, streams flowed eastward from beneath the house's threshold: for the house's front stood toward the east, and the waters flowed from beneath the right side of the house, at the south side of the altar. Then he led me around the way without to the entire gate via the way that looks eastward, and behold, there ran out rivers on the right side. And when the man with the line went eastward, he measured a thousand cubits, and he brought me through the waters, which were up to my ankles. He measured a thousand again and dragged me through the waters, which were up to my knees. He took a thousandth measurement and brought me through; the waves were up to my loins. After that, he measured a thousand, and it was a river that I couldn't cross because the waters had risen, waters that I couldn't swim in, and a river that I couldn't cross. And he says to me, "Hast thou seen this, Son of Man?" Then he brought me to the river's edge and forced me to return. When I returned, I noticed that there were numerous trees on both sides of the river on both sides. Then he said to me, "These rivers issue out toward the east land, and flow down into the desert, and go into the sea; and the waters shall be healed because they are brought forth into the sea." And it shall be so, that everything that lives and moves, wherever the rivers flow, shall live; and there shall be a large multitude of fish, for these waters shall come thither: for they shall be healed; and everything that lives and moves, wherever the river comes, shall live. And it shall come to be that the fishermen shall stand on it from Engedi to Eneglaim, and they shall be a place to spread out nets; their fish shall be according to their sorts, as the fish of the wide sea, exceeding many. The miry regions and marshes, on the other hand, will not be cured; they will be turned into salt. And by the river, on this side and on that side, shall grow all trees for meat, whose leaf shall not fade, nor shall the fruit thereof be consumed: it shall bring forth new fruit according to his months, because their waters issued from the sanctuary: and the fruit thereof shall be for meat, and the leaf thereof for medicine.

The river that runs from the lofty and sacred peak has everything you require. Are you standing in His glory's river? Because water flowed from the sanctuary, from God's throne in heaven, where His presence is, the trees along the river's banks were fertile trees that would not wither, with fruit that would not fail in Ezekiel's vision.

In the river of His glory, you'll find abundant living. You will be frightened by his presence. It will change your life.

24:6 (Psalms) This is the generation of those who seek him, O Jacob, who seek thy face. Selah.

We need the Jacob generation's heart. God is on the lookout for those who have the heart of Jacob. Those saints who hunger for Him, thirst for Him, and follow Him with zeal will be able to stand in and experience His presence.

God's River of Glory will convert you into princes with Him, able to subdue the kingdoms of darkness and demonstrate His power.

God's strength is manifested in those who hunger for Him, not in those who seek His might. He will not use His power to protect our reputation. The resurrection's power is for those who know Him and want to know Him. It's for those who sit at Jesus' feet, those who want nothing more than to be with Him.

Moses is told to leave the mountain and lead the Israelites to the Promised Land in Exodus 33. God tells Moses that He is removing His manifest presence from their midst and that He will not accompany him. He did, however, tell Moses that the fulfillment of His promises, blessings, protection, anointing, and the strength of His hand could still be expected. He even promised that an angel would accompany them as their guide. Moses, on the other hand, was not pleased. He desired to be in God's presence. If I have found grace in your eyes, show Me now Your path that I may know You, he prayed as he set his tent outside the tabernacle.

Some Christians are content with a form of Christianity that emphasizes power, blessings, protection, and anointing.

God is seeking for someone who will say things in the same way that Moses did.

Exodus 33:11 is a passage from the book of Exodus. And the LORD spoke to Moses face to face, as if he were speaking to a friend. And he returned to the tent; however, his servant Joshua, the son of Nun, a young man, did not leave the tabernacle.

Exodus 33:13 is a passage from the book of Exodus. Now, if I have found grace in thine eyes, shew me now thy path, that I may know thee, that I may find grace in thine eyes: and consider that this nation is thy people.

When they already had a good acquaintance and communicated to one other, why would Moses ask to know Him? Moses wasn't content with simply speaking to God; he craved even more of Him. He aspired to have a true understanding of God.

"Show me Your Glory," Moses said. Allow Your brilliance to descend, and in that majesty, reveal yourself to me. Please reveal Your persona to me. Moses rose to a new level as God's brightness fell, and by revelation, he knew God like he had never known God before.

All I teach is through revelation received by God's glory falling upon me when I experienced God's splendor and He began to talk to me in His glory. It's a revelation in which I realize certain things right away. We obtain revelation when we enter the glory realm and function in the environment of heaven. Why would God tell Moses that He was removing His visible presence from the midst of the Israelites? "What made Him say, 'I'm not going with you?'" The golden calf, I feel, is the answer. Even in the actual church, there are idols that aren't pliable to what God wants to do, such as inflexible scheduling. Unfortunately, many churches today are unaware that they lack God's glory, because the Lord's blessing remains, just as it did for the Israelites. But no matter how many people are in a church, conference hall, or crusade grounds, no matter how much force is present, if there is no glory, it's all for naught. Outwardly, everything appears to be in order, but many ministries today are so preoccupied with seeing God fulfill His promises that they fail to notice that God is not present.

Even ministry can get in the way of the Lord. There would be miracles if God's manifest presence was there, since when the glory falls, everything falls. All a church or ministry requires is God's glory. The programs aren't required. It doesn't need to be hyped up.

It doesn't require those items in the natural world as it believes it requires. It is in desperate need of God. People flock to seeker-friendly churches, but if God's evident splendor was there, hundreds of thousands of souls would be saved, and hundreds of thousands of miracles would occur.

"I'm not satisfied, God!" Moses declared. Even if you give me nations, I will not be pleased unless You accompany me. Moses' ministry had reached its pinnacle. This isn't to imply that you shouldn't pray to God for healing, provision, or deliverance. The Lord's strength is with you, and He will heal, bless, and set you free. But what God desires more than anything else is for you to desire Him and be content with Him alone.

Is there an idol in your life that you worship instead of God? An idol is anything that separates us from God. Are you too pre-occupied with yourself to spend time with Him? You must make time for God in some way. I understand that it isn't always easy. Even though I am busy with sermon preparation, preaching, and travel, I must make time for God. You can pour your heart and soul into ministry and witness tremendous acts of God, but without His presence, without Him in our midst, it's all for naught.

God desires for us to be personal with Him, but this intimacy comes with a condition, and that condition is godliness.

24:4, 5 (Psalms) He who has pure hands and a pure heart, who has not lifted up his spirit to vanity or pledged falsely. He will be blessed by the LORD, and the God of his salvation will bless him with righteousness.

God desires that we seek godliness.

12:14 in Hebrews Follow the path of peace with all people and holiness, without which no one will be able to see the Lord:

If you want to enter the glory, you must have clean hands and a pure heart, which is true holiness. True godliness does not consist of you striving to do all the correct things you know you should do on your own. Getting God to manifest in your flesh is true godliness. You will not dare to do those things that you know grieve and harm God's heart when God manifests in your flesh.

3:16 1 Timothy And the secret of godliness is without dispute great: God was visible in the flesh, justified in the Spirit, seen by angels, preached to the Gentiles, believed in the world, and received up into glory.

Godliness is the manifestation of Jesus' splendour in our flesh, so that we begin to appear, talk, and behave like Him in everything we do and say. That is godliness in its purest form. If you have sin in your life, jump into the river and let it wash it away. When we witness His brightness, Jesus will manifest in our flesh.

We are transformed into the image of Jesus when we gaze at his glory, his face.

3:18 (2 Corinthians) But we are all transformed into the same image from glory to glory, exactly as by the Spirit of the Lord, with open faces beholding the glory of the Lord as in a glass. The closer we approach to God, the more His brilliance shines through and exposes our sin.

Do you truly desire to behold His glory?

24:7-9 (Psalms) Lift up your heads, O gates; and be lifted up, ye eternal doors; for the King of glory will enter. Who is this glorious King? The LORD is formidable in battle, strong and mighty. Lift up your heads, O gates; indeed lift them up, ye everlasting doors, for the King of glory will enter.

The King of Glory will come to those who seek Him out. The King of Glory is on his way to those who want holiness, or God in the flesh. The King of Glory will arrive to those who imitate what they see, the manifest image of Christ.

The church is represented by the gates and doors. You are the gateway, the door through which the Lord's splendor will be revealed.

2:14 Habakkuk Because, as the seas cover the sea, the earth will be flooded with knowledge of the LORD's splendor.

People will be able to recognize God. God will be known by the sick, the lost, and the dying. Those who require Jesus will recognize Him. It's all due to His majesty. Who will be the one to release His majesty? Yes, you are! You are the temple, the gate, and the door through which the river of God's splendor flows. Look at His glory, His presence, and then open the gate, open the entrance, and let His glory out.

Hunger for Him and adore Him in holiness' splendor. Renew your attention and enhance your life's glory level!

12

Conclusion

I'm delighted you read this book, whether it was a gift or something you bought yourself.

God's Glory has forever changed my life. Even when you have discovered God's Glory, you must continue to seek more. There is never enough of God's presence. For the past few years, I've been experiencing the Glory, and it's triggered a slew of attacks. I'm not referring to attacks from the outside world, but rather from within the Church. One of my first was religion and tradition, which I thought was awful enough, but it was nothing. My closest friends, as well as those I was grooming for ministry, have turned on me. Through it all, there has been a group of folks who have stood by my side. I'd like to take this occasion to express my gratitude to my colleagues, partners, and friends. All of you that stayed by my side throughout the ordeal.

I want everyone to understand that God's Glory has a cost. The cost will be justified. Things that would typically take months or years happen in a matter of seconds to days in God's Glory. God is the Glory, and we must treasure it.

The Body of Christ is about to see something unprecedented. Prepare yourself for what comes from God's love. I'm excited, and I hope you are as well.

I sense the Lord wants to say something, so here it is: I, the Lord, am sending forth a new wave of my presence. There will be many more waves after this one. At the same time, I'm igniting revival fires across the United States. This has already been sent. Other fires will occur as a result of the fires that have already been ignited. The price of revival will be your lives. When I want to pour forth my Revival Glory, so many of my people choose to stay at home. Despite the fact that my people are not hungry, they still want me to come. My people invite me to visit, but when I arrive, they are not there. Yes, there are a few hungry saints left, but where have all my people gone?

I've been in previous outpourings where the Lord was there, but many of my people didn't like the box I placed it in. I'm about to breach a religious pride, so prepare yourselves. Man-made programs will fade away, and I will begin to lay out my design. Are you ready for me to visit twelve different regions around the United States? I'm going to pour myself out like you've never seen before. My glory will ebb and flow like tidal waves. Anything can happen in the tidal waves of my Glory. Prepare yourselves for new waves of worship, preaching, and signs and wonders. I'm going to go after the youth and shake up my Church's leadership. My preference will be towards the young. Do not belittle your youth. There will be incredible creative marvels, such as the restoration of body weight to Aids and Cancer patients, the growth of arms and legs in paraplegics, and the supernatural removal of metal from people's bodies.

The harvest will continue to grow in size. My harvest season is here.

Milton Keynes UK
Ingram Content Group UK Ltd.
UKHW041832280823
427655UK00003B/36